VOICES OF
AKENFIELD

Ronald
Blythe

English Journeys

PENGUIN BOOKS

Published by the Penguin Group
Penguin Books Ltd, 80 Strand, London WC2R ORL, England
Penguin Group (USA) Inc., 375 Hudson Street, New York, New York 10014, USA
Penguin Group (Canada), 90 Eglinton Avenue East, Suite 700, Toronto, Ontario, Canada M4P 2Y3
(a division of Pearson Penguin Canada Inc.)
Penguin Ireland, 25 St Stephen's Green, Dublin 2, Ireland
(a division of Penguin Books Ltd)
Penguin Group (Australia), 250 Camberwell Road, Camberwell, Victoria 3124, Australia
(a division of Pearson Australia Group Pty Ltd)
Penguin Books India Pvt Ltd, 11 Community Centre, Panchsheel Park, New Delhi – 110 017, India
Penguin Group (NZ), 67 Apollo Drive, Rosedale, Auckland 0632, New Zealand
(a division of Pearson New Zealand Ltd)
Penguin Books (South Africa) (Pty) Ltd, 24 Sturdee Avenue, Rosebank, Johannesburg 2196, South Africa

Penguin Books Ltd, Registered Offices: 80 Strand, London WC2R ORL, England

www.penguin.com

This selection taken from *Akenfield*, first published by Allen Lane 1969
Published in Penguin Books 2009
This special edition for Sandpiper Books / Postscript published 2011

4

All rights reserved

Set by Rowland Phototypesetting Ltd, Bury St Edmunds, Suffolk
Printed in England by Clays Ltd, St Ives plc

ISBN: 978-0-141-19079-2

www.greenpenguin.co.uk

Leonard Thompson · aged seventy-one · farm worker

There were ten of us in the family and as my father was a farm labourer earning 13*s*. a week you can just imagine how we lived. I will tell you the first thing which I can remember. It was when I was three – about 1899. We were all sitting round the fire waiting for my soldier brother to come home – he was the eldest boy in the family. He arrived about six in the evening and had managed to ride all the way from Ipswich station in a milk-cart. This young man came in, and it was the first time I had seen him. He wore a red coat and looked very lively. Mother got up and kissed him but Father just sat and said, 'How are you?' Then we had tea, all of us staring at my brother. It was dark, it was the winter-time. A few days later he walked away and my mother stood right out in the middle of the road, watching. He was going to fight in South Africa. He walked smartly down the lane until his red coat was no bigger than a poppy. Then the tree hid him. We never saw him again. He went all through the war but caught enteric fever afterwards and died. He was twenty-one.

Very soon after this it was very hard living indeed for the family. There were seven children at home and father's wages had been reduced to 10*s*. a week. Our cottage was nearly empty – except for people. There was a scrubbed brick floor and just one rug made of scraps of old clothes pegged into a sack. The cottage had a living-room, a larder and two bedrooms. Six of us boys and girls slept in one bedroom and our parents and the baby slept in the other. There was no newspaper and nothing to read except the Bible. All the village houses were like this.

Our food was apples, potatoes, swedes and bread, and we drank our tea without milk or sugar. Skim milk could be bought from the farm but it was thought a luxury. Nobody could get enough to eat no matter how they tried. Two of my brothers were out to work. One was eight years old and he got 3s. a week, the other got about 7s. Our biggest trouble was water. There was no water near, it all had to be fetched from the foot of a hill nearly a mile away. 'Drink all you can at school', we were told – there was a tap at school. You would see the boys and girls filling themselves up like camels before they left school so that they would have enough water to last the day. I always remember the bitter metal taste of the tap in my mouth; it was cold – beautiful! I remember once coming home from school and feeling almost mad for water. My mother was washing the linen on the doorstep and when her back was turned I swigged two cupfuls from the tub. Up it came at once – it was all soapsuds! Mother did no more than box my ears. That is how they thought about you at that time.

Our parents and all the cottage people were very religious and very patriotic. The patriotic songs and the church hymns seemed equally holy. They took our breath away. The boys marched through the village singing,

Lords Roberts and Kitchener, Generals Buller and
   White,
All dressed in khaki, going out to fight . . .

and their faces would look sincere and important. It was all 'my country' – country, country, country. You heard nothing else. There was no music in the village then except at the chapel or the church and our family liked it so much that we hurried from one to the other to hear all we could. People like us, who went where we fancied on a Sunday, were called 'Devil-dodgers'. We all went to one service after another and ate packets of bread-and-jam in between. People believed in religion then, which I think was a good thing because if they hadn't got religion there would have been a revolution. Nobody would have stuck it. Religion disciplined us and gave us the strength to put up with things. The parson was very respected. He could do what he liked with us when he felt like it. One day he came to our house and told my eldest sister, who was eleven, to leave school. 'I think you needn't finish,' he said. 'You can go and be maid to old Mrs Barney Wickes, now she has lost her husband.' Mrs Barney Wickes was blind and my sister was paid a penny a day out of Parish Relief to look after her.

People were strict. Parents were strict. All the village children thought of was how to get away, how to 'get on'. But we had our games and treats. We had a game called 'Hudney'. A stone was placed on a brick and had to be knocked off by another stone when it was aimed at it. When you ran to retrieve the stone a boy would try and hit you with a ball and if he did you were out of the game. We played this for hours on end. We had no toys, no books and we didn't play cricket or football. But all the boys and young men swam naked in the river in the summertime. It was our biggest happiness. Boys were washed until they were about two, then their bodies didn't see water again until they learned to swim. We didn't look dirty. We were healthy, strong children, but small. One of our great desires was to have cake. Nearly all our food was boiled on account of there being no oven in most of the cottages. A 'treat' was any party where you could eat cake.

I walked two miles to school. There were so many children you could hardly squeeze in the room. All the same, it was very cold in the winter. Most of the boys had suits and boots on with nothing underneath. Every now and then we used to have to stand on the outside of our desks and mark-time to get our circulation back. We did left-right, left-right for about five minutes – good God, what a row we made! Later on, I heard this sound again in Gallipoli. It seemed homely and familiar. We must have been bashing some landing-stage. The school was useless. The farmers came and took boys away from it when they felt like it, the parson raided it for servants. The teacher was a respectable woman who did her best. Sometimes she would bring the *Daily Graphic* down and show us the news. I looked forward to leaving school so that I could get educated. I knew that education was in books, not in school: there were no books there. I was a child when I left but I already knew that our 'learning' was rubbish, that our food was rubbish and that I should end as rubbish if I didn't look out.

When I was six we moved to another house. It was a tied-cottage with a thatched roof and handsome beams. My father said, 'We shall be better off, boys, we shall have a nice spring of water just across the road, and that will be a great relief. Also we shall have a nice big garden with two apple trees, a Doctor Harvey and a Blenheim Orange.' We moved to this house in 1904. As soon as we got there, mother went stone-picking in the fields. She didn't have to do this because we were living in a tied-cottage but because we had to buy some new clothes. We helped her when we got back from school at five o'clock. She had to pick up twenty-four bushels of stones a day to get 2s. Each parish had to mend its own lanes then and the stones were used for this. A tumbril was put in the field and a line was chalked round it. When you had filled it up to the line you got the 2s. It would take the whole day. We did it every minute we weren't at school and all through the holidays. It was all I can remember.

But during the harvest holiday we had a change – gleaning. The women would meet and say, 'Is Scarlets ready for gleaning yet? Is Great Mosses?' – these were the names of the fields. They meant, not has the field been cut but have they cleared the 'policeman'. The policeman was the name given to the last trave or stook which the farmers would leave standing in the middle of the field so they could have time to rake-up all the loose corn they could before the gleaners arrived. There was one farmer who made a habit of keeping the gleaners waiting and one night a young man stole the 'policeman'. The next morning the gleaners hurried in and gleaned masses – the field hadn't been raked, you see. The whole village was laughing – except the farmer. He raked-up quick the next year, I can tell you!

I gleaned all my boyhood. I ran away from it once but came to grief, and since the results have been with me all my life, I will tell you about it. When I was six I got fed up with being in the gleaning-field with all the women, so I ran off to help the boy who worked the cattle-cake machine. In no time my hand was caught and my fingers were squashed. The farmer was just coming up by the granary on his horse when he heard me screaming. 'What have you been up to, you young scamp?' he shouted. 'My fingers – they're in the cake-breaker!' And he said – I shall never forget it – 'Get you off home then!' But when he saw my hand he changed his tune and said, 'Get up to the house'. The farmer's wife tied some rag round my hand and took me home and my mother wheeled me miles to the doctor's in a pram. My sister was home from service, so she came with us and held me while the doctor scraped the grease out of my wounds with a knife, stitched up one finger, cut another, pared it like a stick and tied what was left to the bone, and then moved on to the next finger. I lifted the roof, I can tell you. There was no anaesthetic, nothing. My sister began to faint and the doctor got on to her something terrific. 'Damn silly girl – clear off outside if you can't stand it! Fetch my groom in.' So the groom came and held me until it was finished. All the time the doctor worked he shouted. 'What did you do it for? Why? Damn little nuisance! Stupid little fool!'

Nobody used pity then, and especially not to children, and particularly not to boys. The farmer told my father and he said, 'I'll give him something to think about when I get home!' It was harvest so it was late when he returned. 'Where's that boy Leonard?' he said 'I'm going to give him a good hiding.' 'He's gone to bed, he's had enough,' said mother. My father didn't realize how bad it was, you see. The tops of three of my fingers had been cut off. So he didn't touch me.

There were a lot of hidings then. My father was a good man and didn't like giving them to us, but some people did. Father never smoked or drank, and he looked after his children. He had a wonderful character in the parish. He would go to work with three-quarters of a loaf of bread and a little bit of cheese, and maybe a couple of onions, but when we ran to meet him after his day's work, he would give us the cheese. He had saved it for us. 'I can do without that,' he would say. We were thrashed a lot at school. Fathers would be ordered to the school to hold their sons while the mistress thrashed them. Most of the teachers were big thrashers. But we were tough, very tough. Everybody said, 'don't-don't' to boys then and after awhile we didn't listen. We were wondering how we could get away.

I left school when I was thirteen, on April 20th when the corn was low. I helped my mother pulling up docks in the Big Field for a shilling an acre, which my mother took. She could see that I was too big to have money taken from me like this, so when the farmer came round she said, 'Can't you give my boy a proper job?' She meant a regular job with a wage. But the farmer just laughed and rode away. So the next week I tried my luck at another farm. Mr Wakeling, this farmer, was very tall and he had three sons of about eighteen to twenty-one who were all over six feet. They all stood looking down at me and smiling. 'So you are thirteen and you have left school, but what can you do?' 'I can do anything.' 'Well, there's a mangold field over there – you do that.'

'What are you going to get?' asked my mother when I told her. 'I never asked and he never said,' I replied. It was the beginning of being grown-up.

I had a week in this field, singling mangolds, and I did well because I had often done the job before, after school. The farmer came and looked and said, 'You've done very well, my little man. How much have I got to give you?' 'My mother said half-a-crown but perhaps you would sooner give me a rise.' But the farmer thought half-a-crown was good, which was what I got for sixty hours' work. When the harvest came along, the boy who was doing the milking, and who was seventeen and strong, was told to load corn and I had to take over the cows. The farmer's riding ponies and then his sons' ponies were added. Then the farmer said, 'You'll have to work Sundays now, but I shall be giving you another sixpence.' So I got 3s. a week. Mother said, 'How lucky you are!'

Shortly after this my father came to grief with his farmer and we had to leave the tied-cottage. We moved down by the river and when we were settled father took my brother and myself to his new employer and, twizzling me round so that I could be seen, said, 'Here's a good strong boy. I want 4s. 6d. a week for him.' 'We'll see about that at the end of the week,' said the farmer. Then my father made my brother stand forward – he was fifteen – and said, 'Look what a fine lad. I want 8s. a week for him.' The farmer thought for a minute, looked us up and down and said, 'All right.'

The second week that I was at this new farm I had to drive a herd of cattle to Ipswich. I was thirteen and had lived only ten miles away all my life, but I had never been to this big town before. The farmer went ahead in his trap and waited for me at Ipswich market. He sold the cows and bought some more, and told me to drive them back to the farm. Most of my work was like this, walking cattle along the roads backwards and forwards to the market – about twenty-five miles a day. The farmer was a dealer. I stayed with him a year and four months and was paid 4s. 6d. a week. And then I got into a hell of a row. I'd driven a flock of sheep from Ipswich and the next morning they found that one had died. The farmer was in a terrible stew. He ran down the field and met my mother on her way to chapel and told her all about it. I had driven the sheep too hard, he said. 'And you drive boys too hard!' said my mother – she had no fear at all. Well, the truth of the matter is that she said a lot of things she'd only thought until then, and so I left the farm. It must seem that there was war between farmers and their men in those days. I think there was, particularly in Suffolk. These employers were famous for their meanness. They took all they could from the men and boys who worked their land. They bought their life's strength for as little as they could. They wore us out without a thought because, with the big families, there was a continuous supply of labour. Fourteen young men left the village in 1909–11 to join the army. There wasn't a recruiting drive, they just escaped. And some people just changed their sky, as they say, and I was one of them.

Every week in the *Suffolk Chronicle and Mercury* there was an advertisement which said, 'Lads for Yorkshire. Milk or Ploughing. Good Homes. Fares Paid. Apply: Woods of Stowmarket.' All the Yorkshire farm-workers, you see, had left the land to work in the factories and mills. So they hit on this idea of getting workers up from Suffolk, where things were desperate, to cultivate the Yorkshire farms. So I thought, right, I'll go! I was getting 9s. a week for a seventy-five-hour week in a cowshed. I had four hours off a week, from 10–2 on a Sunday. So I went to Yorkshire. I met Mr Woods on Bury St Edmunds station and he gave me my ticket. I went to a farm in the West Riding. It was the first time I had been away from home. I lived in a little old room on the farm with two other boys and was told that I would get £12 at the end of the year, which was 5s. a week, but also my food and keep. The food was good; we ate it with the servant in the kitchen. We worked like little donkeys until we were a bit unsteady on our feet, then it was bed. Then work. I had to pay a pound a year to an old woman to do my washing, pay a pound to get home again and a pound for boots and corduroys, but I came to Suffolk with eight golden sovereigns in my hand and felt a millionaire.

I returned to my old farm at Akenfield for 11s. a week, but I was unsettled. When the farmer stopped my pay because it was raining and we couldn't thrash, I said to my seventeen-year-old mate, 'Bugger him. We'll go off and join the army.' It was March 4th 1914. We joined the army a few hours after we had made our decision. We walked to Ipswich and got the train to Colchester. We were soaked to the skin but very happy. At the barracks we kissed the Bible and were given a shilling. The recruiting sergeant said, 'You can't go home in all this rain, you can sleep in a bed in the recruiting room'. In the morning he said, 'Go home and say good-bye, and here's ten shillings each for your food and fares. Report back on Monday.'

In my four months' training with the regiment I put on nearly a stone in weight and got a bit taller. They said it was the food but it was really because for the first time in my life there had been no strenuous work. I want to say this simply as a fact, that village people in Suffolk in my day were worked to death. It literally happened. It is not a figure of speech. I was worked mercilessly. I am not complaining about it. It is what happened to me.

We were all delighted when war broke out on August 4th. I was now a machine-gunner in the Third Essex Regiment. A lot of boys from the village were with me and although we were all sleeping in ditches at Harwich, wrapped in our greatcoats, we were bursting with happiness. We were all damned glad to have got off the farms. I had 7s. a week and sent my mother half of it. If you did this, the government would add another 3s. 6d. – so my

mother got 7s. My father died early this year and my
mother lived on this 7s. a week for the whole of the war,
adding a scrap to it by doing washing, and weeding in
the fields. Neither of my parents lived long enough to
draw the Old Age Pension. I can remember, when work
was short, a group of unemployed young men coming
to where some old men were sugar-beeting, which is
the worst job there is, and shouting, 'Now that you
grandfathers have got the pension' – it was 5s. a week –
'why don't you get out of the field and give us a chance?'
These 'old' men were only in their fifties but the hardness
of their lives had made them ancient.

All this trouble with the village fell behind us now. I
was nineteen and off to the Dardanelles, which is the
Hellespont, I discovered. I had two boys from the village
with me. We'd heard a lot about France so we thought
we'd try Turkey. The band played on the banks of the
river as we pulled out of Plymouth and I wondered if
we would ever come home again. We were all so patriotic then and had been taught to love England in a fierce
kind of way. The village wasn't England; England was
something better than the village. We got to Gib and it
was lovely and warm. Naked Spanish boys dived round
us for coins. There were about fifty nurses on the top
deck and they threw tanners. You could see they were
having an eye-opener. We stopped to coal-up. The dust
blew all over the decks and all over us. We were packed
like sardines and eating rubbish again. Water and salt
porridge for breakfast. Beans and high salt pork for
dinner. The pork was too bad for land-men to eat so we
threw it into the coaldust and the coolies snatched it up

and thrust it into their mouths, or put it into sacks to take home for their families.

We arrived at the Dardanelles and saw the guns flashing and heard the rifle-fire. They heaved our ship, the *River Clyde*, right up to the shore. They had cut a hole in it and made a little pier, so we were able to walk straight off and on to the beach. We all sat there – on the Hellespont! – waiting for it to get light. The first things we saw were big wrecked Turkish guns, the second a big marquee. It didn't make me think of the military but of the village fêtes. Other people must have thought like this because I remember how we all rushed up to it, like boys getting into a circus, and then found it all laced up. We unlaced it and rushed in. It was full of corpses. Dead Englishmen, lines and lines of them, and with their eyes wide open. We all stopped talking. I'd never seen a dead man before and here I was looking at two or three hundred of them. It was our first fear. Nobody had mentioned this. I was very shocked. I thought of Suffolk and it seemed a happy place for the first time.

Later that day we marched through open country and came to within a mile and half of the front line. It was incredible. We were there – at the war! The place we had reached was called 'dead ground' because it was where the enemy couldn't see you. We lay in little square holes, myself next to James Sears from the village. He was about thirty and married. That evening we wandered about on the dead ground and asked about friends of ours who had arrived a month or so ago. 'How is Ernie Taylor?' – 'Ernie? – he's gone.' 'Have you seen Albert Paternoster?' – 'Albert? – he's gone.' We learned that if 300 had 'gone' but 700 were left, then this wasn't too bad. We then knew how unimportant our names were.

I was on sentry that night. A chap named Scott told me that I must only put my head up for a second but that in this time I must see as much as I could. Every third man along the trench was a sentry. The next night we had to move on to the third line of trenches and we heard that the Gurkhas were going over and that we had to support their rear. But when we got to the communication trench we found it so full of dead men that we could hardly move. Their faces were quite black and you couldn't tell Turk from English. There was the most terrible stink and for a while there was nothing but the living being sick on to the dead. I did sentry again that night. It was one-two-sentry, one-two-sentry all along the trench, as before. I knew the next sentry up quite well. I remembered him in Suffolk singing to his horses as he ploughed. Now he fell back with a great scream and a look of surprise – dead. It is quick, anyway, I thought. On June 4th we went over the top. We took the Turks' trench and held it. It was called Hill 13. The next day we were relieved and told to rest for three hours, but it wasn't more than half an hour before the relieving regiment came running back. The Turks had returned and recaptured their trench. On June 6th my favourite officer was killed and no end of us butchered, but we managed to get hold of Hill 13 again. We found a great muddle, carnage and men without rifles shouting '*Allah! Allah!*', which is God's name in the Turkish language. Of the sixty men I had started out to war from Harwich with, there were only three left.

We set to work to bury people. We pushed them into the sides of the trench but bits of them kept getting uncovered and sticking out, like people in a badly made bed. Hands were the worst; they would escape from the sand, pointing, begging – even waving! There was one which we all shook when we passed, saying, 'Good morning', in a posh voice. Everybody did it. The bottom of the trench was springy like a mattress because of all the bodies underneath. At night, when the stench was worse, we tied crêpe round our mouths and noses. This crêpe had been given to us because it was supposed to prevent us being gassed. The flies entered the trenches at night and lined them completely with a density which was like moving cloth. We killed millions by slapping our spades along the trench walls but the next night it would be just as bad. We were all lousy and we couldn't stop shitting because we had caught dysentery. We wept, not because we were frightened but because we were so dirty.

We didn't feel indignant against the Government. We believed all they said, all the propaganda. We believed the fighting had got to be done. We were fighting for England. You only had to say 'England' to stop any argument. We shot and shot. On August 6th they made a landing at Suvla Bay and we took Hill 13 again, and with very few casualties this time. We'd done a good job. The trench had been lost yet again, you see. When we got back for the third time we found a little length of trench which had somehow missed the bombardment.

There were about six Turkish boys in it and we butchered them right quick. We couldn't stay in the trench, we had to go on. Then we ran into machine-gun fire and had to fall flat in the heather, or whatever it was. Suddenly my mate caught fire as he lay there. A bullet had hit his ammunition belt. Several people near jumped up and ran back, away from the burning man and the machine-gun fire. I could hear the strike of the gun about a foot above my head. I lay between the burning man and a friend of mine called Darky Fowler. Darky used to be a shepherd Helmingham way. I put my hand out and shook him, and said, 'Darky, we've got to go back. We *must* go back!' He never answered. He had gone. I lay there thinking how funny it was that I should end my life that night. Then my mate began to go off like a firework – the fire was exploding his cartridges. That did it! I up and ran.

There is nobody can say that you have killed a man. I shot through so many because I was a machine-gunner. Did they all die? – I don't know. You got very frightened of the murdering and you did sometimes think, 'What is all this about? What is it for?' But mostly you were thinking of how to stay alive. The more the killing, the more you thought about living. You felt brave and honoured that you should be fighting for England. You knew that all the people at home were for it. We believed we were fighting for a good cause and so, I expect, did the Turks. You didn't think personally. You can't get on with wars if you think personally. You can't say you *shot* a man, although you know you hit him, because there were so many guns going at the same time. But I should think that I killed several. [Several means quite a few or many in Suffolk.]

After Gallipoli I went to France. I went through the Somme and through the battle of Arras, after which I was captured. It was 14th April 1917. We ran and gave ourselves up, there was nothing more we could do. The Germans lined us up and marched us off. I thought, 'We're safe now. We're out of it . . .' I didn't know what was going to happen. If I had I would sooner have gone through all the fighting again. It was the worst thing which ever happened to me in my life. We were taken to Lille, where the Germans had to make us ill and wretched in a week in order to march us through the town, so that they could say to the people, 'Look at the great British army, look what it has been reduced to!' We were driven into dark dungeons, straight off the battlefield, starved, made filthy and in only *six days* we were ill and we looked like scarecrows. The Germans knew how to do this to men. After the parade about 300 of us were packed into a half-built mansion and there we lived on pearl barley boiled in coppers and bread or cake made of weed-seed. Then we were put into a forest to make charcoal and sometimes the Germans shot into our legs as we marched. We never knew what they would do next. They chose boys to thrash. I don't know why I was chosen but I was a favourite for this thrashing and was always being taken off for a beating. George Holmes, a farmer's son from the village, was one of the people who died from the ill-treatment.

At Christmas 1917 they took us to Germany, right down to Kiel. It was snowing and we were in rags. No shoes. They gave us wooden clogs. We dug on the Kiel railway, making a track to the Baltic for the big guns. Many people died. On November 5th 1918 some German sailors arrived and set us free. They cut all the barbed wire and left just one guard in charge. 'You can leave if you like,' they said. 'The war will soon be over. There is going to be a revolution, so keep off the roads. You could go and help the farmers pick up potatoes. That would be sensible.'

So this is what we did. And when the war ended, there we were, Germans, Poles, Russians and Englishmen, working in the fields and realizing that there was damn little growing in them.

The soldiers who got back to the village recovered very quickly. People who had lost their sons felt strange. Generally speaking, we were thankful that it was all over and we could get back to our work. Yet things *had* changed and people were different. The farm-workers who had been soldiers were looked at in a new way. There were a few more privileges around than there used to be. They'd let you take a rabbit or two, for instance. Before 1914, if you'd caught a rabbit, my God, the world would have come to an end! The sack was the least you'd get. We felt that there must be no slipping back to the bad old ways and about 1920 we formed a branch of the Agricultural Labourers' Union.

[. . .]

It took a brave man to show his politics in Suffolk all through the 1930s. If you weren't a Tory you were a troublemaker. All the same, we got the Union going again in 1934. Things changed after this, first very slowly, then faster and faster.

I am old now. I read library books about the Great War – my war. The one I am reading now is called *The Sword-Bearers*. I have these deep lines on my face because I have worked under fierce suns.

Emily Leggett · aged seventy-nine · horseman's widow

I have been wed and widowed twice. My first husband was head horseman at Round Wood Farm and when we married his wages were 13s. a week. He used to give me 12s. and keep a bob for his pocket. We were children together, then lovers, then I married him. He lived in the next door double-dweller. We were both nineteen when we wed. A beautiful boy he was. It seems a long time now since I saw him. He had six horses to look after and he used to get up at five o'clock every morning to bait* them.

When the war came he was sent at once to join the cavalry at Curragh Camp in Ireland because he was such a fine horseman. He was trained there for about three months and then he was given three days' leave before going to the Western front. But the water was so rough that he only had one day and one night with me. That was the only time I saw him between his joining-up and his going. One day he was blown off his horse and blown

---

* Feed.

to pieces. There was nothing of him left to find. So he hasn't got a grave. The chaplain wrote and told me all about it. When the telegram came and I read of his death I couldn't possibly believe it. I couldn't think that it was true. My poor young husband! I had only just got his last letter – I still have it. It said not to worry. He was just twenty-five.

I was born in this house, so was my father and his father. It is a charity house – or was – we have to pay rent and rates now. Nearly all the people I used to know are gone. I went to school here – what little I went. I was blinded by eye ulcers a lot of my childhood and so I didn't do much schooling. We took our poorness naturally. We knew within a little what we were going to get and that there would never be any more. So that was that. My father was one of eight and I've often heard him say that he didn't know what it was like to have a new pair of shoes on his feet. He only had shoes which other folk passed on to him. We ought to be thankful to be as we are today. Whatever would our poor old mothers and fathers have thought if they could see all the money we get now! We know that it doesn't go far but we touch it.

I can remember the men mowing by hand, twenty-four of them in the one field, and each behind the other. The children helped in their own way. We started field work when we were five or six. I used to carry my father's food to the harvest field. It would be crowded with men and when they saw the food they would laugh and cheer. The farmers gave each man two bushels of malt and a pound of hops for doing the harvest. They would have cost 6*s*. if you had to buy them. Then they got £5 or £5 10*s*. largess or bonus when it was all over. The quicker they got the harvest in the more money they got. Of course they worked all hours God ever made to get this money. My father would go to the beanfield at two in the morning to get the beans when they were dew-damp, so that they didn't shell-out. Just when there was enough light to see. People now get as many pounds in the week as they got shillings!

We women and children went gleaning when the last wagons had left the field. We picked up the corn for mother and she cut the ears off with her pig-knife and put them in a sack. We were allowed to keep all this. We fed it to the fowls or ground it into flour.

A lot of people shared bedrooms in those days – I mean four and five to a room because of the big families. We never saw anything wrong. People think we did but we didn't. My sister and me and my brother shared a room until we married but we knew nothing. I'm sure of this. Today they hear too much about sex too early. My father was church-warden and a good man. He never went to bed without kneeling against his chair and saying his prayers.

After I had been a widow for five years I married Bob – another horseman! We had no children of our own but we brought up a foster-daughter. We managed all right although it was hard. I walked ten miles, there and back, to Woodbridge every Friday for the shopping, and if it was a dry summer, so that the pond disappeared, I walked two miles there and back for a couple of pails of water. This water came from a spring and it was a treat after the pond, I can tell you! Worth going after. The dust from the roads in the summertime was enough to blind you and if it rained the mud squirted up into your long skirts and made them filthy. People got very dirty then.

When the second war came it changed the village more than it had ever been changed before, or so I believe. It was because they sent the Irishmen to build the aerodrome. Blackies as well. Hundreds of Irish and Blackies concreted the fields. They got the stones for the concrete from Shingle Street. Two of the Irish boys were billeted on me because I had two bedrooms. The Germans came to bomb the aerodrome and when this happened the Irishmen used to run outside and stand in the pond! Me and my husband we sat in our chairs and waited. Things would fall off the mantelpiece and the village would shake. It was awful.

My husband began to be ill then. On the days when I had to take him into Ipswich for treatment I always came back to find the tea ready. The Irishmen had done it. I have been blessed with beautiful boys.

My second husband had an awful death – worse than the first I sometimes think. I never had my clothes off except for washing for twenty weeks. I never left him for an hour. The doctor wanted me to have him put away – they always do – but I said no. Men should die where they have lived. The nurse came in and washed him every day. It didn't cost me nothing. So I saw the end of him. He died on the Friday and was buried on the Sunday because he was a bad corpse. It was cancer of the throat. The war was over then and they were smashing up the aerodrome and putting back the corn. 'I shan't live to see it,' he said. And he didn't. Nobody could have wished for two better husbands. My horse-men – both gone!

Fred Mitchell · *aged eighty-five* · *horseman*

I worked with horses. I came from the West. Have you been to Chedburgh – Wickhambrook way? I came from that direction. I lived there two years. Then I lived at Whepstead – have you been to Whepstead? I had a few years along of a farmer there – horseman, machinery man and most everything else. The farmer was a big chapel man from Clare. Do you know Clare? Then on I moved. To Poslingford. Do you know Poslingford? That's a rum old village. It was there that I met the farmer who brought me to the East and brought me bad luck, as it happened. The farmer had a hold of me. You see, the Great War broke out and he got exempts for me, one after another, until it was all over, so he had me.

I was living at Depden when I first started ploughing. The farmer said to me, 'You're going to plough today'. I was something pleased. The horses were in the stable. I soon got hold of them and off I went! I was fifteen years old and I had been at work for seven years. I kept about on this Depden farm – do you know Depden? – for one year and then, after the harvest, I thought I'd have a go at Newmarket. Newmarket was crowded with village boys who had a handy way with horses. They hoped the toffs would fancy them and put them in the racing stables. I soon found a job there; it was to do with the heavy horses. The man who employed me would cart anything anywhere. He'd got over fifty horses, including a pair of blacks for funerals, a pair of greys for weddings, and everything up to date. Yes, I've been about – but it hasn't done me much good. The trouble is, I shouldn't have met this Poslingford farmer, then I could have gone on getting about.

I saw the big change. My father worked on a farm – and his father. They both got very near to ninety, I believe. They were hardy old sorts. They never had a thing amiss with them. They worked and lived, and then kind of toppled over at the end. I should have been like them but my accident made the difference to me. The horses ran away with me on the farm. It was only two fields away from this house. It was a terrible accident; it jagged me all to pieces. The horses bolted in the field and ruined me. We were using the self-binder at the time. It was the second year I was in this village and thirty-eight year ago or more. I was at the top of the field whole and then at the bottom of the field broken, and all in minutes. I should not have come here. I wasn't in the hospital much more than a month. They sent me out on stilts. Hang on, they said, you'll soon manage. Today, if you've only got a finger-ache they'll let you stay comfortable until it's better. I wasn't half looked after. They had to lift me out of the hospital to get me home. 'Have you got a nurse?' they said. 'I don't know of one,' I said. 'Oh, dear,' they said. 'Then however will you get on?' I had to be massaged but nobody I knew could do that kind of thing for me. So my leg healed but became short and walking on it has wrung me over. It hurts me a bit all the time. But still, I'm lucky to be alive!

I got no compensation at all. My governor, being a tidy well-off farmer, made my club money up to my wages, but of course there was the family and they were all young. I had a rough old time from then on, I can tell you! But I pulled through. I've got to eighty-five in spite of it all. They tell me I don't look it.

I had a struggle to bring the family up. You had to nearly perish to bring a family up then. It was too much. There wasn't a penny for nothing. They have money now, don't they? We didn't have money. I never had no good times. Nothing began to happen until my boys were all grown up and I was getting old. But there, I wasn't the only one! The farmers were sharp with us. If you couldn't do a job you were reminded that plenty more could. So you had to be careful. I had to accept everything my governor said to me. I learnt never to answer a word. I dursn't say nothing. Today you can be a man with men, but not then. That is how it was. It will never be like that again. I lived when other men could do what they liked with me. We feared so much. We even feared the weather! Today a farmer must pay for the week, whatever the weather. But we were always being sent home. We dreaded the rain; it washed our few shillings away.

I have this invalid-chair now. I had a three-wheel bike up to a few years ago but it got harder and harder to push it along. Then this chair came. The village had bought it for me – they all clubbed together like. The young men made them do it, I'm told. So perhaps it isn't such a bad village after all. It must have cost pounds and these boys just gave it to me. These boys play a lot. Look up any time and ten-to-one you'll find them playing. Football, riding around. I never did any playing in all my life. There was nothing in my childhood, only work. I never had pleasure. One day a year I went to Felixstowe along with the chapel women and children, and that was my pleasure. But I have forgotten one thing – the singing. There was such a lot of singing in the villages then, and this was my pleasure, too. Boys sang in the fields, and at night we all met at the Forge and sang. The chapels were full of singing. When the first war came, it was singing, singing all the time. So I lie; I have had pleasure. I have had singing.

[. . .]

Samuel Gissing · aged eighty · retired farm worker

SAM'S SONG

It is late on Saturday night, virtually the eleventh hour, and the pub roars its contentment. One or two say they are going to make an early night of it but they don't make a move. In fact, nobody moves. They stand or sit in controlled, cautious clusters, talking their heads off but somehow rooted to the spot. A note of warning wavers in the blare of conversation and when somebody – obviously a drunken fool – shouts, 'Come on, Sammy,

let's be hearin' you!' there are nervous pleas of, 'Quiet
... quiet ...' 'Come on, Sam!' shouts the fool again, but
Sam doesn't look up or react in any way whatsoever.
He, too, is talking hard and apparently unable to make
head or tail of what is going on. His neighbour is turned
to stone. Smoke crawls along the beams. A boy reaches
towards the one-armed bandit, then controls himself.
The landlord takes up the attitude of a priest, hands
resting wide apart on the bar, head glorified by the glitter
of doilies, mirrors and miniature bottles festooned with
fairy lights. Mysteriously, for there is no commotion, a
space appears in the middle of the room, a ring of
worn flagstones littered with matches, ash and beer
spots. Still nobody looks at Sam and he talks steadily on
to his friend, who now has the worried expression of a
man entrusted with a key role. The uproar now becomes
less casual-seeming. Eyes search for 'young' Hickey, who
is forty-ish and waiting his cue. He rises.

'Good night, Hickey,' somebody says provocatively.

'Good night to *you*,' Hickey returns in a voice which
means, 'If you bugger things up at this stage I'll kill
you'.

He then dances. His suede shoes slap lightly on the
paving and his tie jumps out of his waistcoat. His hair
hangs away from his bald patch in a big flap. He dances
with his back to Sam, who at first ignores him and then
begins to watch the tripping flutter of Hickey's feet with
a kind of pity. Hickey, the enticer, now breaks into a fast
soft, clopping step, then breaks down, slaps his thigh and
begins again. He does very well but gives up with a 'It's
no good. I can't keep it up, you see ...'

'*Hickey!*' shriek the women on the settles in affected outrage.

The landlord holds up a large white hand as though he is going to give a blessing, but it falls on the light-switch panel. Sam stands up, buttoning his jacket, emptying his glass. He could be leaving – even when he reaches the bare floor he could be on his way home. But he stops, stretches like a wiry old cat, makes himself tall – and dances. His eyes blaze in the firelight. Huge polished boots fly. The dance is a kind of kicking stamp, coltish, vigorous. Sam's heel-irons actually produce sparks and this makes everybody laugh. He dances and dances, eventually clasping his hands nonchalantly behind his back with a gesture of, 'Stop me when you've had enough . . .' Nobody does and he has to stop himself, which happens in the midst of a crescendo of stamping. His body resumes its old slightly bent position gratefully and heaves with breath. The applause is solemn, a patter of clapping – no shouts. Young Hickey then opens his melodeon with a great yawning chord and Sam sings his song, with difficulty at first because he hasn't got his puff back, then with surprising strength. Like his dance, Sam's song is violent, full of attack. Nobody joins in though 'several' know the words backwards.

> There was a man lived in the West,
>   Limbo clashmo!
> There was a man lived in the West,
>   He married the woman that he liked best.
> With a ricararo, ricararo, milk in the morn
>   O' dary mingo.

He married this woman and brought her home,
    Limbo clashmo!
He married this woman and brought her home,
And set her in his best parlour room,
With a ricararo, ricararo, milk in the morn
    O' dary mingo.

My man and I went to the fold,
    Limbo clashmo!
My man and I went to the fold,
And caught the finest wether that we could
    hold,
With a ricararo, ricararo, milk in the morn
    O'dary mingo.

We fleeced this wether and brought him home,
    Limbo clashmo!
We fleeced this wether and brought him home,
Says I, Wife, now you've begun your doom,
With a ricararo, ricararo, milk in the morn
    O'dary mingo.

I laid this skin on my wife's back,
    Limbo clashmo!
I laid this skin on my wife's back,
And on to it I then did swack,
With a ricararo, ricararo, milk in the morn
    O'dary mingo.

I painted her with ashen oil
    Limbo clashmo!

I painted her with ashen oil,
 Till she could both bake, brew, wash and boil,
With a ricararo, ricararo, milk in the morn
 O'dary mingo . . . mingo.

John Grout · aged eighty-eight · farmer

I have farmed in Akenfield since 1926. I had 135 acres
and didn't use a tractor until 1952, and then I never
got on with the thing. I have been a man without
machinery, as you might say. I was born near Campsey
Ash and worked for my father as a child. I did the cows.
He was a man who didn't like cows, so I did them. Then
I went to school. My father had five labourers who got
9s. a week but he always gave them a shilling extra when
they got wed.

Nobody really saw money then, though that didn't
mean that they didn't want to see it. I wanted to see it
so much that I applied for a job on the railway. A
'situation', they called it, and they weren't so far wrong
– it was a situation all right. Whatever could I have been
thinking about! A relation of mine spoke for me and
soon I was working at Broad Street Station near Liver-
pool Street. There were lots of Suffolk men working
there and hardly any mortal one of them ever got home
again. They all wanted to get home, they were that sad
in London. And their big wages were little there. Some
ran away to Canada and were never heard of again. They
couldn't write, you see; that is how they got lost. There

was a place in Broad Street Station where you can stare through the arches and see the stars, and they were the only things I can remember seeing in London. That is the truth.

I stayed ten months and then I got home. I wouldn't go back to my father's farm, I got a job with Lord Rendlesham. He was a rare big gentleman in the neighbourhood and was famous for his horses. Why, he kept three men who did nothing else but see after the stallions. There were scores of horses – mostly shires and punches. The greatest of these was a punch stallion called Big Boy who had won so many brass medals he couldn't carry them all on his harness. Men came from all over to see these horses but they hardly ever saw Big Boy. He was hid up and not to be looked at.

The head horseman was called the 'lord' – and that's what he was, lord of all the horses. That was me one day, I was the lord of the horses. The place ran like clockwork. All the harnessing was done in strict order, first this, then that. The ploughing teams left and returned to the stable yards according to the rank of the ploughman. If you happened to get back before someone senior to you, you just had to wait in the lane until he had arrived. *Then* you could go, but not before.

The horses were friends and loved like men. Some men would do more for a horse than they would for a wife. The ploughmen talked softly to their teams all day long and you could see the horses listening. Although the teams ploughed twenty yards apart, the men didn't talk much to each other, except sometimes they sang.

Each man ploughed in his own fashion and with his own mark. It looked all the same if you didn't know about ploughing, but a farmer could walk on a field ploughed by ten different teams and tell which bit was ploughed by which. Sometimes he would pay a penny an acre extra for perfect ploughing. Or he would make a deal with the ploughman – 'free rent for good work'. That could mean £5 a year. The men worked perfectly to get this, but they also worked perfectly because it was *their* work. It belonged to them. It was theirs.

The plough-teams left for the field at seven sharp in the morning and finished at three in the afternoon. They reckoned a ploughman would walk eleven miles a day on average. It wasn't hard walking in the dirt, not like the rough roads. The horsemen were the big men on the farm. They kept in with each other and had secrets. They were a whispering lot. If someone who wasn't a ploughman came upon them and they happened to be talking, they'd soon change the conversation! And if you disturbed them in a room where the horse medicine was, it was covered up double quick. They made the horses obey with a sniff from a rag which they kept in their pockets. Caraway seeds had something to do with it, I believe, although others say different.

A lot of farmers hid their horses during the Great War, when the officers came round. The officers always gave good money for a horse but sometimes the horses were like brothers and the men couldn't let them go, so they hid them. I wasn't called up. Nothing happened to me and I didn't remind them. We didn't really miss the men who didn't come back. The village stayed the same.

If there were changes, I never felt them, so I can't remark on them. There was still no money about. People seemed to live without it. They also lived without the Church. I'm sorry about this but it is true. I hardly ever went when I was young. The holy time was the harvest. Just before it began, the farmer would call his men together and say, 'Tell me your harvest bargain'. So the men chose a harvest lord who told the farmer how much they wanted to get the harvest in, and then master and lord shook hands on the bargain.

We reaped by hand. You could count thirty mowers in the same field, each followed by his partner, who did the sheaving. The mowers used their own scythes and were very particular about them. They cost 7s. 6d. in Wickham Market, but it wasn't the buying of them, it was the keeping them sharp. You would get a man who could never learn to sharpen, no matter how he tried. A mate might help him, but then he might not. Some men mowed so quick they just fled through the corn all the day long. Each mower took eleven rows of corn on his blade, no more and no less. We were allowed seventeen pints of beer a day each and none of this beer might leave the field once it had been brought. What was left each day had to be kept and drunk before eight on a Saturday night. It was all home-brewed beer and was made like this:

You boiled five or six pails of water in a copper. Then you took one pail of the boiling water and one pail of cold water and added them together in a tub big enough to hold eighteen gallons. You then added a bushel of malt to the water in the tub. You then added boiling water from the copper until there was eighteen gallons in all in the tub. Cover up and keep warm and leave standing for at least seven hours, although the longer the better. When it has stood, fill the copper three parts full from the tub, boil for an hour and add half a pound of hops. Then empty into a second tub. Repeat with the rest. All the beer should now be in one tub and covered with a sack and allowed to cool. But before this, take a little of the warm beer in a basin add two ounces of yeast and let it stand for the night. Add this to the main tub in the morning, then cask the beer. You can drink it after a week. And it won't be like anything you can taste at the Crown, either.

The lord sat atop of the last load to leave the field and then the women and children came to glean the stubble. Master would then kill a couple of sheep for the Horkey supper and afterwards we all went shouting home. Shouting in the empty old fields – I don't know why. But that's what we did. We'd shout so loud that the boys in the next village would shout back.

Stacking was the next job, all very handsome they had to be – handsome as a building. Then thrashing. It was always reckoned you had to thrash a stack in a day. There wasn't any rest after the harvest. The year had begun again, you see.

Robert Palgrave · aged fifty-five · bellringer,
tower captain

During the war, in 1916, the parson here had two daughters who did a bit of ringing. I once saw them what they
call 'raise the bell', that is bring it full circle. So one day
I went into the church and climbed the belfry, wound a
sack round the clapper, went downstairs – and pulled!
To my amazement I got the bell up, so then I started
practising. That is how I first came to ring. I then brought
other boys to the tower and taught them how to do it,
and then one day we all walked to Burgh and rang the
six bells there. After this we hurried off to Hasketon and
rang the bells there – we couldn't stop. A ringer is first
attracted by the sound of the bells, then he comes to see
how it is done and something quite different gets a hold
of him. Some people say it is the science of the thing.

What a ringer needs most is not strength but the
ability to keep time. Everybody must be dead-on with
their pulls. Nobody must be uneven. You must bring
these two things together in your mind and let them rest
there for ever – bells and time, bells and time. When I
first started the young men were so keen to ring that
they would be lucky to get five minutes' practice each –
so many of them wanted to have a go. We would think
nothing of walking six or more miles just to have a
five-minute practice ring in a good tower. And I have
walked between twenty and thirty miles in a day to ring
a peal of 5,000 changes. All the ringers were great walkers
and you would meet them in bands strolling across

Suffolk from tower to tower. Many of the old ringers couldn't read or write, yet they turned out to be really famous bell-composers and conductors. They could get hundreds of rows of figures into their heads and put them all into practice when they reached the belfry. They could set all the bells ringing wherever they went and bring them all back to 1–2–3–4–5–6–7–8.

The bells tolled for death when I was a boy. It was three times three for a man and three times two for a woman. People would look up and say, 'Hullo, a death?' Then the years of the dead person's age would be tolled and if the bell went on speaking, 'seventy-one, seventy-two . . .' people would say, 'Well, they had a good innings!' But when the bell stopped at eighteen or twenty a hush would come over the fields. People were supposed to pray for the departed soul, and some of them may have done. This practice was continued up until the Second World War, when all the bells of England were silenced. It was never revived. The sexton got a shilling for ringing the death-bell.

I left the village when I was eighteen and went into the guards, which meant Windsor and London. I met the ringers in these places and became very accomplished. I think I can say this without being boastful. I have been a regular ringer ever since. It is such a fascinating art, you see. I know all the bells in Suffolk – and other counties, too, for that matter. I think I have just passed my two thousandth tower. Cathedrals, minsters, priories, abbeys, churches and the secular bells at Windsor Castle, I have rung them all.

Ringing requires a lot more mental than physical

application, particularly now when the modern bell-composers create such wonderful changes and the bells are hung so beautifully they don't need great strength to move them. But of course you have to be fit to be able to swing a bell for two or three hours at a stretch and 'put it in its place', as we say. You also have to be bitten by the bug. You have to be smitten. If you are a real ringer you think about bells morning, noon and night, and you only live for the next time you can have a go at them. You have your ringing books and a lot of study at home. An old ringer at Hasketon told me, 'You must learn it at home and ring it in the tower.'

One of the fascinating things about ringing is that there are about 5,500 peals of bells in the British Isles, ranging from rings of five to peals of twelve. So, you see, you can travel to the towers all your life and still find something new. The towers have a great effect on the sound of the bells which hang in them. The tower here is soft red brick and it absorbs the strike notes, whereas in a modern tower made of concrete and steel you would get a harsh bell note. The old bricks soak up the sound and sweeten it. The taller the tower, the quieter the bells in the village itself. The shorter, the louder. Nowadays, the tendency is to hang the bells about twelve feet lower than the louvres in the belfry windows, so that the noise can come up and then go out across the land. The notes of the bells are distributed evenly. Some towers 'burl out', as we say, and it can be most unpleasant. If you want to stop burling you have to board or brick the windows up until only a small opening is left at the top.

The average weight of a bell in Suffolk is about eleven

hundredweight – as against the tenor bell in St Paul's Cathedral, which is sixty-two hundredweight. When we say 'ring of bells' we mean towers where there are peals of five, six, eight, ten and twelve bells. An eleven hundredweight bell would be the largest of these. People are very attached to old bells because they have spoken for the village so long and are its angel voices, or because they listened to them when they were courting and were young and happy. But I have to reluctantly say that, for those who understand bells, modern bells are best because they have been scientifically tuned. Much of the old bell-making was a hit-or-miss affair. The bell-makers were like a woman with a cake who could turn out four or five passable efforts to every one which was perfect. It was just the same with the bell metal. If it was poured too hot it would split the bell, and if it was too cold it would spoil it. But with a thermometer the modern bellman knows exactly when to pour his metal. He also has instruments to tune his bell 100 per cent perfect. A new bell today is in tune with itself as well as with the other bells in its peal. A bell can be in the key of D but it will still contain many other tones and a bell-founder of today will know how to get rid of these other tones. In the old days a man would cast many bells of the same dimension and yet no two would be alike. It was rule of thumb. And it is just a myth that a silver coin was put in the bell metal because all bell metal, now as then, is about two-thirds copper and one-third tin – and nothing more. Tuning was then done by chipping at the inside of the bell to flatten the tone and chipping at the edge to sharpen it. But it was all very hit and miss.

Too many chips might come off – or not enough – and the bell-founder had only his ear to guide him. Now we trim the bell to agree with a tuning machine. The old bell-founders were itinerate workers. When a village wanted bells they would bring their tools to the church-yard, dig a pit and make a furnace. The bell core was baked whole and then the outer cope was made. More metal was poured into the space between the inner core and the cope. When it was cool, the top was either lifted off or broken off, and there was your bell in its crude state. Then came the tuning and the hanging. It was a great business. One of the finest bells in the world is in Suffolk. It is the Lavenham tenor which Miles Gray made in 1625. It is known to be the sweetest bell in England.

Most of the bell-frames round here are between four and five hundred years old but if they are replaced iron and steel is used, not wood. A bell-frame must be absolutely rigid otherwise it will affect the swinging of the bell and hurt the ringer. The towers sway a lot during the peals. Most of the Suffolk towers sway tremendously, particularly St Mary's at Woodbridge. The vibration of the bells is said to fracture the towers but architects will laugh at this and say it is rubbish.

Before change-ringing came in, bells were used just to make great grave sounds on important occasions, or simply jangled. Then Fabian Stedman evolved a system by which they could be used to make real music. His method is still the most popular today. It is one which is rung on odd numbers of bells – on five, seven, nine or eleven bells. But there has to be an even number of bells to ring it, which sounds rather paradoxical. In other words, you ring 'Stedman' on the front five bells with the largest bell, called the tenor, covering. It would be 2–1–4–3–5 with the tenor bell coming in behind. It produces the best music. After Stedman died, the country people amused themselves by making variations on his method until, all over England, there was a great rage for ringing. The names of men who made important attempts to ring Grandsire Triples, Bob Major, Stedman Caters, Tittum Bob Royal, etc. were painted on boards and hung up in the towers. The great Suffolk ringers were the Chenerys from Wilby, the Banisters from Woolpit and the Baileys from Leiston. The Baileys were eleven brothers and they were ringing in the towers round here just before the Great War. Six other brothers, the Wightmans from Framsden, were ringing at the same time. They rang a seven method Minor peal at Monewdon on March 18th 1914. They had to take their father with them to do this, of course.

The maximum number of changes which can be rung on eight bells is 40,320. This is called 'accomplishing the extent' and it was accomplished on the foundry bells at Loughborough. It took seventeen hours, fifty-nine minutes. It presented a challenge, you see, just as Everest presented a challenge to our friend Hillary. If you are the conductor of a peal you have in your mind a picture of how those bells have to be kept going without one single change repeating itself. And so at intervals the conductor has to make a call which changes the work of the bells.

The ringers are now able to do far more than what was possible forty years ago or more. Some of their sons have been to the university and have applied their mathematical brain power to the art. My youngest son is a most brilliant ringer and probably one of the greatest ringers in the world. He is a mathematician and he was getting things out on paper when he was five years old. He went to the village school, then to the grammar school and then to the university. Nothing ever came difficult to him. He conducts and composes. Where bells are concerned there is nothing he cannot do.

There are new ringing methods composed all the time but people who are not ringers do not hear the tunes. I should say that ninety-nine per cent of the people just hear 'bells ringing'. That is all. Many first-class ringers are tone-deaf and the bells to them are just a noise. It is all figures to them. But when I hear the bells I think, my goodness, how beautiful! How wonderful! The combinations of sounds delight me. If you read the peal boards in the Suffolk towers you will be reading the names of many happy men.

Christopher Falconer · aged thirty-nine · gardener

I went to Lordship's when I was fourteen and stayed for fourteen years. There were seven gardeners and goodness knows how many servants in the house. It was a frightening experience for a boy. Lord and Ladyship were very, very Victorian and very domineering. It was 'swing your arms' every time they saw us. Ladyship would appear suddenly from nowhere when one of us boys were walking off to fetch something. 'Swing your arms!' she would shout. We wore green baize aprons and collars and ties, no matter how hot it was, and whatever we had to do had to be done on the dot. Nobody was allowed to smoke. A gardener was immediately sacked if he was caught smoking, no matter how long he had worked there.

We must never be seen from the house; it was forbidden. And if people were sitting on the terrace or on the lawn, and you had a great barrow-load of weeds, you might have to push it as much as a mile to keep out of view. If you were seen you were always told about it and warned, and as you walked away Ladyship would call after you, 'Swing your arms!' It was terrible. You felt like somebody with a disease.

The boy under-gardeners had to help arrange the flowers in the house. These were done every day. We had to creep in early in the morning before breakfast and replace great banks of flowers in the main rooms. Lordship and Ladyship must never hear or see you doing it; fresh flowers had to just be there, that was all there was to it. There was never a dead flower. It was as if flowers, for them, lived for ever. It was part of the magic in their lives. But the arrangements were how they wanted them and if one of the gardeners had used his imagination, Ladyship noticed at once and soon put a stop to it! The guests always complimented her on the flowers and she always accepted the praise as though she had grown, picked and arranged them herself. It was logical because servants were just part of the machinery of the big house and people don't thank machines, they just keep them trim and working. Or that's how I look at it.

As the years went by, we young men found ourselves being able to talk to Lordship and Ladyship. 'Never speak to them – not one word and no matter how urgent – until they speak to you,' the head-gardener told me on my first day. Ladyship drove about the grounds in a motorchair and would have run us over rather than have to say, 'get out the way'. We must never look at her and she never looked at us. It was the same in the house. If a maid was in a passage and Lordship or Ladyship happened to come along, she would have to face the wall and stand perfectly still until they had passed. I wouldn't think that they felt anything about their servants. We were just there because we were necessary, like water from the tap. We had to listen for voices. If we heard them in a certain walk, we had to make a detour, if not it was, 'But why weren't you listening?' and 'Be alert, boy!' and, when you had been dismissed, 'Swing your arms!'

The garden was huge. The pleasure grounds alone, and not including the park, covered seven acres. The kind of gardening we did there is not seen nowadays. It was a perfect art. Topiary, there was a lot of that. It was a very responsible job. You had only to make one bad clip and a pheasant became a duck. The gardeners usually made up these creatures themselves. We were tempted to cut out something terrible sometimes, so that it grew and grew . . . but of course we never did. Even when we went on to mechanical hedge-trimmers we still kept on topiary. There was a great pride in it, and in hedge-cutting of every sort. It was the hedge which set the garden off and all the big houses competed with each other. Fences were marvellous things, too; there were more than two miles of them round Lordship's and not a pale which wasn't exact. The hedges had tops like billiard-tables. It was get down and have a look, and stand back and have a look. No hedge was left until it was marvellous. There were so many things which really had no need to be done but which we did out of a kind of obstinate pleasure. The asparagus beds in winter were an example. We'd spend hours getting the sides of the clamps absolutely flat and absolutely at a 45° angle, although an ordinary heap of earth would have done just as well.

None of the village people were allowed into the garden. Definitely not. Tradespeople came to their door and never saw the main gardens. Work in front of the house had to be done secretly. About seven in the morning we would tiptoe about the terrace, sweeping the leaves, tying things up, never making a sound, so that nobody in the bedrooms could hear the work being done. This is what luxury means – perfect consideration. We gave, they took. It was the complete arrangement. This is luxury.

Of course, they spent a terrific amount of money on the house and garden. It was the machinery they had to have in order to live. So they kept it going, as you might say. A bad servant was just a bad part and was exchanged for a good part as soon as possible. I thought of this when I was doing my National Service as a fitter in the Tank Corps. It made sense. Yet I got so that I didn't know quite what to think about it all. It was obviously wrong, yet because Lordship and Ladyship were old and had never known any other kind of life, I suppose I felt sorry for them. I always had to give more than was necessary. I couldn't resist it. It was exciting somehow. But when I got home I would be angry with myself. The butler would sometimes come to the pub and imitate them. Laugh – you should have heard us! But I would feel strange inside, pitying and hating at the same time. His favourite joke was:

LADYSHIP: 'Shall we ask the So-and-Sos to luncheon, Bertie?' Silence, then, 'Can they play bridge? Will they like my garden?'
LADYSHIP: 'No, I don't think so.'
LORDSHIP: 'Then don't have 'em.'

Lordship was a friend of King George V. He was a terribly nice man – a real gentleman. A lot of royalty came down from time to time and Lordship and Ladyship were sometimes at Sandringham. The Queen (Queen Elizabeth the Queen Mother) came. She treated us very well and loved the garden. She would tell us boys what they ate for luncheon and then we'd all laugh. The Princess Royal was just the same – easy. But Members of Parliament always imitated Lordship and Ladyship and treated us like fittings. I was amazed by the Royalty. I imagined a bigger kind of Ladyship, but definitely not.

It was strange coming back to the big house after the Tank Corps. I was married now and we had an estate cottage without inside water, a bath or electricity, although it was very pretty and we were very happy. At first, that is. Until Ladyship said that my wife must work in the big house. My wife didn't understand what it would mean. She came from Ilford and had never seen anything like it. She got worried and then she got migraine. The doctor told her that she must leave her work at the big house because it was making her anxious and ill. I told Ladyship, who said, 'But she must come.' I told her what the doctor had said but she just drove to the cottage and told my wife, 'You must come back to the kitchen – do you understand? You *must*.' So that is why we went away. I felt sorry for my wife and for Ladyship; they had no way of knowing each other.

The big house helped me in my life and changed me. Being in private service has educated me. I can talk to anybody. There is one thing about Suffolk folk and that is that they find talk terribly difficult. I don't. I have learned to talk. But working for Lordship made me a foreigner in the village. Those who remain with their own calibre in the village stay in the village family. I belonged to the big-house family and it was hard to leave. I saw the last of the big house while it was self-supporting. Everything, milk, cream, butter, game, fish, flowers, chicory, endive, melons, they were all there behind the hedges. Whatever Lordship and Ladyship wished for, they asked for, and it was brought.

I had a great training as a gardener and acquired all my knowledge completely free. Although I was often horrified by the way we were all treated, I know I got a terrific amount out of it. It is a gardening background which few people now have, and scarcely anybody of my age. In a great garden you grow from the seed and then you see the plant growing where it will always grow, but in a nursery garden it is just produce and sell, produce and sell. Nothing remains. A private gardener like myself would never get on in nursery work because I have had the fine art of tidiness drummed into me. I work privately and could have a choice of twelve or fifteen jobs, all with houses. There is no kind of gardening I can't do. I am not boasting, it is a fact.

How can you describe this anxiety we have about our gardens in Suffolk? I have been to Scotland and they don't have it there. Are gardens our pride? I think so: it is a breeding in the Suffolk people. I have never thought about this before but now I would like to get to the bottom of it. We are all obviously urged to do it as a great necessity in our lives. It is my life. I would die in the attempt to produce a plant, a flower, and bring it to perfection. You take my employer. She never goes abroad. All her holiday imagination is put into her garden. She prefers this to a seven days' wonder. Another thing, I think, which you can put the gardening urge down to is simply ownership. It is wonderful to realize that a beautiful plant is yours. Suffolk people love you to go and boast their gardens. If people want to be polite, the first thing they say is, 'What a beautiful garden'. If a man is clipping a hedge, you must compliment him on it. Hedges have to be praised. This is where the old employers went wrong, they didn't understand about praise. If there had been more praise for gardeners there would still be plenty of good gardeners around. An industrial worker would sooner have a £5 note but a countryman must have praise.

There are a tremendous number of people who garden morning, noon and night and can't begin to be got out of their gardens, but they are a different calibre to myself. They are ex-army officers, ex-naval officers. About seventy per cent of the gardens open to the public in East Anglia belong to ex-military men. I think it must be something to do with time and order. They love complete order and nobody can stop them imposing it on a garden. There must be something in this because I have thought about it a lot. So many of my employer's friends are middle-aged army officers, retired, and they are all fascinated by horticulture. The things which they will do to make a garden is astounding. I've known them to drive all the way to Wiltshire to pick up a stone sink. You see, gardening allows them to go on having routine, order, tidiness, straight edges, upright posts. You can be strict in a garden. They were fantastically strict in the Tank Corps barracks. And tidy! 'If it doesn't move, whitewash it,' they used to say. You look at the names belonging to the National Gardens Scheme and you'll find it's three-quarters officers. And how they work! Although if they're going to have a garden and going to have a good one they have hardly got any alternative. I know a colonel near here who, when he opens his garden for the National Gardens Scheme, has all his machines and tools on display. All the mowers, barrows, spades – everything – are polished and oiled and lined up! You wouldn't have got Lordship doing a daft thing like that – but then you wouldn't have got Lordship letting Tom, Dick and Harry into the park, let alone into the gardens.

The village gardens aren't as good as they used to be

for the very simple reason that a man can go to work for an hour or two extra and earn enough money to buy vegetables for a week, whereas, if he grows them, he's got to dig, buy seed, sow, hoe, water, worry, take up and I don't know what – and all for something he can buy for a few bob. There's not time, anyway, because probably he is out to work, fruit-picking and that sort of thing, and so it is easier for them both to have a packet of frozen peas handy. Life now is much less elaborate and, consequently, much less interesting. As a qualified judge of flowers, I would like to say that Akenfield is more horticultural-minded than it used to be, but it is not, and this is the truth. Not the ordinary village worker. But then you have only to go the next step higher, the salesman in his new bungalow, and it's a very different story. Their gardening is a form of ownership and 'getting on'. They garden neatly. They don't know the difference between tidiness and neatness. They buy expensive ugly things. Their gardens look like shopping. These are the new gardeners who are making the nurserymen rich. It is not the young farm-worker – I wish it was.

The young boys in the village won't touch the garden. They earn too much money as far as I can see. They don't pay enough for what they are learning. I had to help my father in the garden when I was a boy; there was nothing else to do. It was expected of me. You wouldn't get a boy to do this now. You just can't reach the boy. I have cousins in the village only just ten years younger than myself and I can't connect or talk to them. I can talk to educated boys, that is different. They are

not changing. Supposing I wanted to talk about horticulture, it wouldn't do for me to talk to a village boy
of about seventeen from the council houses. I'd be
much better if I went over to Framlingham College and
talked to a seventeen-year-old there. The boy from the
village seems to have no interest in anything. That is
why the village garden is in decline. But the gardening
industry is booming. You have only to go round the
nurseries at the week-end – all the car parks are absolutely full. But not with proper village people. The cars
belong to suburban folk. They are intelligent and lively.
They are busy with gardens, boats and holidays. They
buy very different things to the old country chap who
spent no more on his garden than the price of a packet
of carrot seed.

I have been judging village flower shows and gardens
for nearly ten years, and am one of the officials of the
Village Produce Association. There are branches all over
the country and Suffolk is actually a very poor one. It is
an organization run by the Rural Community Council.
Each judge – there are about forty of us in Suffolk –
attends about a dozen flower shows during the season.
It is very progressive and professional; the old-time ama-
teur judge is out. The shows, and gardening itself, are
spoilt by the tendency to try and grow the biggest vegetable or flower. People are not nearly so keen on the
professional exhibiting side of things in Suffolk as they
are in Yorkshire, for instance. They are more interested
in Suffolk in being the first to have peas or potatoes, or
whatever it is. The great thing is to produce something

before your neighbour does. Real gardening is dying, dying . . . dying. There aren't many gardeners of my calibre left. I am a young man who has got caught in the old ways. I am thirty-nine and I am a Victorian gardener, and this is why the world is strange to me.

Gregory Gladwell · *aged forty-four* · *blacksmith*

Nineteen-nineteen was the year my grandfather had to shut down the forge. He never went back to it. I used to walk by it, eyeing it and thinking. But nothing was rosy wherever you looked. Nearly everybody went out of business. Nothing was sold. People who had left school began to think about the Big House. You realized that it was there, with all the gardeners, grooms and maids and food. You have to face it, the Big House was then an asset to the village. It paid us to raise our hats, which is why we did it. I hear people run the gentry down now but they were better than the farmers in a crisis. Theirs was the only hand which fed us which we could see. So we bowed a bit; it cost nothing, even if it wasn't all courtesy. Nobody left, nobody went away. People were content. However hard up they were, they stayed content. The boys had the arse out of their trousers, no socks and the toes out of their boots. My brothers and myself were like this, yet so happy. I think other families were the same. The village kept close.

The biggest change which I have seen in Akenfield is the growth of discontent. Greed. Nobody ever said,

'Bugger you, Jack, my head is out!' when I was a boy. When you wanted help it was given. It was 'Thank you very much', and that was that. You mustn't pay. It was good enough for a row if you offered to pay. Payment was a crime. This was how things were when I told my parents that I wanted to go into the family business. My grandfather had died and my grandmother was paying a man to open the forge and try and do some trade. My father couldn't afford to pay the apprenticeship fee of half-a-crown a week, so I had to do another job as well. I worked from eight to five at the forge and then three more hours night and morning for a man who kept 160 pigs. I was paid a-penny-a-pig-a-week to feed and clean them out. They weren't the little old things you get today, they were big pigs. Enormous . . . 30–35 stone apiece. The pigman used to pay me when the pigs went to market. It would sometimes come to £5 10s., which was a tidy fortune.

It was all agricultural work at the forge. Mostly shoeing. All the horses were still with us and at seventeen I was shoeing an average of eight horses a day. I remember making my first horseshoe. I started work at the forge on August 2nd and I made this shoe on August 4th. They put you straight into the collar in those days! There was no messing about. When you got a job you began doing it right away. You were expected to catch on quick.

The man my grandmother allowed to run the forge was old and when I was just over seventeen he retired, and I had to carry on alone. I now had to do every mortal thing myself. What I didn't know I had to find out or make up. There was nobody to ask. It was a terrible job, but there, we got over it. It was still all farm work, of course. Mostly shoeing. The horseman would stand at the head while the work was being done, so that was a bit of help. He could hold it like. I was such a thin little lad it was a masterpiece how I could hold anything! There was no thought of what you might call art-and-craft work, only plough counters, harrows, door-hinges and such farm things. There was no money about; everybody was bare-poor. I charged 6s. 8d. to put four shoes on a horse. I reckoned that with a quiet horse with good feet the task would take an hour. I hardly made a profit. There are still plenty of horses round here, of course – hunt horses, pony-club horses – it is most unusual for a village to have so many of them around. And I don't mind shoeing them. The trouble is that people who have these kind of horses reckon on you shoeing them for next to nothing. I won't do that. Not now. If people will pay what I charge and won't grumble, then I'll shoe for them, but not otherwise. I am supposed to have served a five-year apprenticeship, and if work isn't worth a little when you've done that, then blast them. I won't mess after it. I remember how hard it was to make myself free, for that is what I was really up to when I was here all alone before the war. I don't know what it is, I can't explain it, but you see I am the only one out of all my family – and there are five of us brothers – who had any intention of coming to the smithy. My brothers couldn't have cared less about the place. I wanted to come, *had* to come. But it is silly to be sentimental. What I sometimes think is that I am my grandfather, an old one. It is the truth when I say that I can sit in the shop of a

Sunday, smoking my pipe, and be as happy as if I were sitting in the house. I wasn't born soon enough, that is the trouble. By rights, I should be dead and gone. I think like the old people. I have a tendency to do what I want to do, if the maggot bites. However pressing matters are, I do what I fancy. I think, probably, my attitude could be wrong. We have our pressures now with bills and bank managers and book-keeping, but I say to myself, this is not the highest thing; this is business. You are a tradesman; this is the highest thing. Making, doing. I feel I should have lived during the 1700s. That would have done me. But I am losing my place, aren't I?

Well, the war came, and one or two German prisoners came to help me out. They were pleasant lads. When they went back I had a boy from the army school, after he had finished his training. He had been an army apprentice farrier and I finished him off. When he left, one or two more arrived and for the first time in my life I had a few minutes to spare, so I began to amuse myself by making ornamental things. I entered one or two competitions and won prizes. And then, after the war, this wonderful thing happened, I married. The business was steady now. I had over a hundred horses on my books which had to be shod three times a year, which meant that I was making 1,200 shoes a year. Of course, the horses were passing, but so slowly that it didn't seem possible that they were soon to disappear off the farms for ever. I still saw the things I sent to the crafts section of the Suffolk Show as a hobby. I couldn't imagine living by such work.

Then new people came and bought up the old houses.

They'd spend a mint of money 'putting it all back as it was'. They couldn't buy the things they needed for the restoration; they hadn't been made for donkey's years. So I had to start making them again. My wife went round, keeping her eye open for bolts, latches, handles, grates; drawing them and finding out their dates, and I made more of them as exactly as you're not likely to tell the difference. Mind you, it took time. It took all hours. But it was a fine thing for me to have something lying on the bench before me made by one of the old men, and my hands doing again what his had done.

[. . .]

I think I am a dedicated man. I won't have financial trouble – I mean, to hell with it! I won't have life all spoilt by money. I don't worry about dying, although I am mid-way through, but I dread being old and unable to work. We are all living in the rat-race, however far out in the wilds we are. The village is so quiet now. Nobody walks about in it. You don't say you saw your neighbour, you say you passed his car. People wave and toot where they used to talk. They're all out for what they can get. Nobody goes to look at what somebody else has done and have a chat about it. If you saw somebody ploughing or clearing the marsh, you used to meet up with a neighbour and say, 'Let's go and see what he's up to.'

I talk to the boys. I train them in 'steps'. The oldest is twenty-two now and doesn't want much supervising. But the others are fifteen and seventeen and you have to watch them. I treat them as individuals. There's young Den, if you said something amiss to him it would upset him so much you wouldn't do nothing with him for a week. Big as an ox and soft as a girl. He is a great tradesman already. But Robin, you have to swear at him regular once a month, or you wouldn't do anything with him. If those two boys had been apprenticed together, you would have made a man of one and offended the other – or vice versa. You must never offend a boy. I always look at the parents before I take an apprentice. If you know the home, you already know the son.

I'm against sport. I hate it. If work and sport changed places, this country wouldn't be in a muddle. Sport and holidays have become a mania, an insanity. If anybody wanted a holiday, I wouldn't stop them from taking one, but I hate holidays as much as I hate sport, and that's saying something. These boys won't be like me; they'll never work as I have worked – and perhaps they shouldn't have to. I've been working two pieces of metal together on the anvil with the sledge-hammer, when my vest caught fire and I daren't pause to put it out! When two men were working, hitting the anvil in turn, they would get each other's sparks. You would be open right down the front and they flew against your nakedness. A blacksmith always rolls his shirtsleeves under, so the sparks don't lodge in the folds. Now, with the emery sparks, we have to watch out for eye-trouble.

[. . .]

Jubal Merton · aged sixty · wheelwright and blacksmith

I've lived in the village all my life. I've never been away. I left school in 1922, when I was thirteen, and was apprenticed to my father and my uncle, who owned these premises. My father was the wheelwright and my uncle was the blacksmith. I was the only apprentice and they were very strict. 'You've got to have a good eye,' they said. 'Everything that's got to be done in wheel-wrighting has got to be done by the eye. You've got to let your eye be your guide.' They were right, of course. What we do here isn't like ordinary carpenter's work. When you get the hub of a wheel it has to be morticed once and only once first go.

The first job I had to do was to make spokes, and sometimes I was allowed to saw out the shafts for the tumbrils. All the shafts were cut out by handsaw from heavy planks of wood about 3½ inches thick and about two feet wide. We planed these and shaped them up fine. Heaps of times I did a shaft and I'd think, 'That's lovely!' Then my father would rub his hand up it and say, 'Why, boy, it ain't *half* done!' He was a first-class wheelwright and was known all over Suffolk, and my grandfather and great-grandfather were the same. They all worked in this same shop and the wagons they made lie about in the farmyards. They ain't used but they can't wear out. When I got so that I could use a plane and a wheel-shave, I started to make wheelbarrows. They were a difficult job, a most difficult job indeed. Especially the front pieces which we called the stumps. The stump was another thing you had to cut right first time else it was no good. There was no second chance in so much of what we did. It made us cautious but at the same time it made us willing to take a risk. It was as much in the eye as in the hand. There was a moment when you had to say *now*! Then you could breathe again.

One of the most exacting things was making the fellies [fellows] for the wheel. There would be six fellies and when they were put together they made the rim of the wheel. These were all cut out by an old bow-saw which belonged to my grandfather and the inner part shaped with an adze. They were made of ash and the wheel-wright always chose roadside trees for his fellies. He'd never touch a low-meadow ash because that wouldn't do at all. Of course, ash that grew down by the river was lovely timber to use, but a wheelwright would never use it. He went to the hedges, where the wood was tough and hard. He'd walk through the lanes and note the ashes and when he saw a good one, he'd buy it, cut it down and let it lie in the ditch for a couple of years until the bark fell off. Then it was ready. He also looked for shaft wood. If you look at the ash trees you'll find that many of their boughs grow in the shape of shafts. When my father saw a good shaft shape a-growing, he'd keep his eye on it until it was just the right size to cut and plane. Then he'd have it.

For making the hubs we always chose wych-elm. A wych-elm twists in the growth and it is impossible to split it. You cut the hub out of a ring of the trunk and fixed the fellies to it by twelve spokes. The bodywork of the wagons was made of oak, although some farmers had a fancy for poplar wood because you couldn't scratch splinters out of poplar with a rake. It was the old English white poplar which they fancied.

When I had helped to make a wagon I had to learn to paint it. We did everything in this shop, you see. The farmers were most particular about the painting. The colours were all bought in Ipswich. There was red lead and vegetable black, white lead, which was like thick distemper, and there was Chinese red and Venetian red, all these were the old colours used by the wagon-makers. The bodywork was all painted blue. Always blue. The blue rode well in the corn. The wheels were done in Chinese red and lined-out with Venetian red, which was marvellously expensive – about £1 an ounce. We mixed all the paints here. Paint for small jobs was ground on a little stone but if we had a lot to do we ground it in a paint-mill. Nothing whatever was wasted of anything. You had to grind paint very, very slowly so that the mill didn't warm-up. If it did it would discolour the paint. The farmers were very proud of their wagons and tumbrils and would wash them down every week-end. Some of them had to go to Ipswich two or three times a week and they had to look fine. A tumbril could travel with about two tons a time. They were beautiful and they had to be kept beautiful. They weren't very expensive. My father made tumbrils for £12 a time when he was a young man. When I first started making them they cost £25 – that is a one-horse tumbril. A wagon would cost about £40. Once they were finished they lasted for ever.

The village was full of wagons a hundred years old or more when I was a boy, and still perfect.

[. . .]

Ernie Bowers · aged fifty-five · thatcher

I started thatching along with my dad at the age of fourteen. This would be round about 1929. My dad had been a thatcher ever since his boyhood. He left school when he was eleven and went along with the local thatcher and he picked the trade up off him. There was a great lot of thatching in those days, you can be sure. And there was plenty of straw to do it with, although straw is rare stuff now.

A thatcher then would have two boys to help him through the summer-time but after October he'd just have the one. The other was stood off and had to fend for himself until the summer came round again. That is how it was. In those days it was seasonal work for some. There would be plenty of rick-thatching then, of course. The farmer would come along and say, 'We've got a couple of ricks want doing. You be along early.' And we were along early, I can tell you – five o'clock most likely. And we'd have done two ricks by midday. Then we would go back to our building job.

I was nineteen when I started on my own. My dad said, 'Well, son, it's up to you now.' It was our parting. That was all he said. I had two boys like the others and I was out on my own. That is how we worked it. The farmers didn't let the farm labourers do the thatching, they always came to us. It was different in Norfolk, where they'd let anybody do a stack. But in East Suffolk it was a special job and my father and myself, working apart with our two boys each, would thatch anything up to 600 ricks a year. We charged according to the size of the rick. Some ricks would be nine yards long by five yards wide, some would be ten by eleven, some twelve by six and some thirteen by seven. When the rick-thatching season was on you would go round and measure your work up and make out your accounts.

Every parish had its own thatcher in the 1920s. But in the 1930s things changed. Most of the good thatchers were getting on the old side and beginning to drop out. I can remember five or six great thatchers of the old school dying then. Nobody replaced them. They were men of the old time – of the old life. They didn't teach their craft to apprentices, they would just pick up the odd man who was walking around on the dole and ask him to give them a hand. They wouldn't teach this man anything. It was a bad time and people were losing heart, I suppose. There wasn't the money about and everything was terrible. Those who didn't see it couldn't believe it. I would be cycling more than fifteen miles to do a job, and in all weathers. There was skimping on the food. We didn't have anything and we couldn't get anything. It was impossible. People have quite forgotten what it was like not to be able to get things. I spent 1s. 6d. a week on my pleasures and gave everything else to Mother. But I got to know the things about the thatching trade which only the old men knew. I can remember the first house

I thatched on my own and the first rick. I did the rick alone because my dad fell ill. I was seventeen and it was a stack of reeds at the Church Farm, Campsey Ash. The reeds had been cut and brought up from Alde river at Snape. Thatching reeds is a painful job and plays merry hell with your hands. They were thatched at Campsey to keep them dry until they could be used to mend the barn roof. Reeds are like everything else, you just can't cut them and lay them in a heap and leave them. They have to be cared for. We like reeds which grow in brackish water best. We like them to grow in the brack caused by the salt tides meeting the river waters every twelve hours. They're pickled a bit, I suppose.

I never worked on a farm and was glad of it. I was my own man. The farmers round here treated their men shameful before the war and none of us forgets this. I've seen a lad only two minutes late who'd be told to 'take the rest of the day off and come back in the morning'. They had to be so careful. There was always somebody waiting at the gate to take their place. I wasn't on the farm but I saw it all. And now it's, 'Oh dear, oh dear, the poor old farmer! He can't afford nothing but he has a new car every year. Oh dear, oh dear!'

Thatching was very cheap when I was young. Labour was cheap, everything was cheap. My father would re-lay a ten-foot square of roof for £1 and think that he was earning money! Today, a job like that would cost £30 and to thatch the roof of an ordinary cottage will cost between £4–£500. But you must remember that you are getting a sixty-year roof – a marvellous, beautiful roof, warm in winter, cool in summer – for this price. There is nothing like it. A thatch is wind-proof, frost-proof and good to look at. I cock my eye up at thatches I did twenty years past and watch them getting better and better. I strip right down to the rafters before I start – although some won't. They'll pile on and pile on. Eventually, like too much sewing of a pair of shoes which brings a pulling away from the welt, the thatch begins to slip off. We did a job at Bacton last year where so much straw had been piled on to the roof over the years that it just fell into the house and the owner had to put a complete new roof on. Most of the old houses still have their original rafters. All of oak, they are and very, very old. I make a roof thatch fourteen inches thick, whether it is straw or reed. The reeds are driven into position with a legget, which is a flat piece of board covered with horseshoe nails and set on a handle at an angle. Cruel work, it is. You start at the bottom of the roof and move upwards till you reach the crown, driving the bundles of reeds into position and fastening them to hazel rods which you cut in the woods during the winter. We use hazel because it is the best splitting wood there is and the best to get a point on. Then comes the pattern. We all have our own pattern; it is our signature, you might say. A thatcher can look at a roof and tell you who thatched it by the pattern.

There used to be special patterns and decorations for the stacks years ago, particularly for the round stacks. There were three kinds of stacks, the round, the boat-shaped and the gable-end, and the stack-yard was a nice place, I can tell you – very handsome. They were a way of decorating the village when the harvest was over and great pride went into putting them up. They were set where they could be seen from the farmhouse and from the road, so that they could be looked at and enjoyed. My dad always set a great sheaf of fine ears at the top of his round stacks and very nice they looked.

I work as we used to work. I stop thatching about the middle of December and spend the winter bushing-up. These are the four months when I'm not earning a halfpenny. Just collecting material. I have to search for wheat and rye straw from farms where they aren't using a combine. Thatching straw must be drum-thrashed and barley and oat straw is no use at all. I have to search the woods for hazel branches and cut them into lengths and cut the reeds from the marshes. This is the only cut you make on the reed, the one cut when you take it from the river. Thatching is very popular now and I am teaching the craft to my brother's son, who is eighteen. He'll carry on. I shall have to teach one of my boys too.

I get up at half past five of a morning. I work many hours. I get tired, but I will be all right, I suppose. There are all these great boys in the house – they keep you lively. But you can't get into conversation with a young person as you could years ago. They just haven't got the interest. They don't want our kind of talk. They're all strangers – all strangers.

Horry Rose · aged sixty-one · saddler

[. . .]

I lost my father when I was nine, so I had to think about work. In those days families didn't have money and boys hurried to work as early as they could so they could earn something. I thought I would be a harness-maker. There was this saddler's shop, you see, right in front of our cottage and a new plate-glass window had been fixed over the small panes of the old window, so you saw the saddlers at work in the lamp-light behind the double window. The scene took my eye. I used to long to be inside the window and working away there with the men. It all looked so peaceful and secure. When I was 12½ I forced myself to go inside and talk to the owner, Mr Peterson – 'Knacker' Peterson was what this gentleman was called – and I told him how I had watched him at work and how I would like to be like him. He listened and then said, 'Very well, I'll take you on. I will give you sixpence a week.'

I wasn't a bound apprentice. I worked a four-year apprenticeship and then one year as an improver. I worked from seven till seven each day and after I became fourteen I got 1s. a week. The war had just started and there was a lot to do, and soon the old gentleman was giving me eighteen-pence a week. Two saddlers were called up and that left only the foreman and myself, which meant that I had to do man's work. So my wages rose to 5s. – which wasn't man's money. My mother said, 'Well, you can't help it; you've got to honour the arrangement and put up with it.' It was never a very highly paid job for anybody. A journeyman got £1 a week and the foreman a shilling extra. The old gentleman didn't die a rich man but he had his satisfactions. After you had got a job you thought less about what you were paid for it than you did in perfecting what you had to do. No matter how many times a young craftsman did his work wrong or badly, his boss could afford to say, 'Do that again.' Time was money, but such small money as made no difference. We had to 'honour bargains' – it was a religious law amongst the tradesmen. The old gentleman used to say, 'Horry, if you bargain to do a job for a price, do you do it for that price – even if it takes longer than you thought and you lose a little money. You'll get the customer's good-will, and you'll also learn a sharp lesson on under-estimating time when you have to make another deal.' We had our customers for life. I will say this for the Suffolk farmers, that if you gave them a good deal, they'd stay by you for always. We lived by loyalty.

We also said that the farmers were bad payers, but that was because they hadn't got the money. They were having a bad time like everybody else. The Scotch farmers who came here in the 1930s were really good payers. They worked harder, farmed better – and paid. Their wives helped them. Too many of the Suffolk farmers' wives were trying to be ladies.

The saddler's shop has only been in three hands since 1840. The first owner was a Mr Lyon and he sold it to my old gentleman, and I bought it from him. I got it in

1930. I employed three apprentices but it was a dying trade. I could have done with more boys but they wouldn't come to work for me if they could get anything else. Our trade came from what was known as 'heavy work' which we did for the horse farms. I felt things changing as far back as 1920 and was tempted to leave the village and go to work in Newmarket, but it so happened that my mother was ill. So I lost my chance to go away. Whether I should have been any better off or more satisfied I don't know. I should have done racehorse work. I was a craftsman here and I would have been a craftsman there, so perhaps it would not have been so much of a change.

The shop has always been the largest village saddlers and harness-makers in this area. We have had a long run. It used to be from dead horse to live horse, as you might say, because the leather we used to make harness from came from the hides of horses we slaughtered in the knacker's yard behind the shop. That is why the old gentleman was called Knacker Peterson: it was his common name. There is a rope walk behind the shop where ropes for the farms were made from local flax. They laid the strands out along the walk and then twisted them up. The walls of the rope walk are covered with dozens of little marks, about an inch long. These were the tallies made by a boy called the 'scratcher'. Every time a length of rope was laid in the walk, he marked it up. So you see the business has always been changing.

Our leather was bought from a tannery in Ipswich – W. & A. J. Turner's in the Bromford Road. We bought black harness backs for heavy work, light brown backs for brown-work and we had special mule hide for making the great straps for mills, thrashing machines and such like. Our shop had quite a name for making these belts. It was very, very hard work. Some of our material came from a tannery near Stowmarket. Everything we used was bought locally. Horse-hide is harsh stuff. It is used for special jobs such as heavy glove-making. We called cow-hide 'neats' hide. Neats is the old word for cattle. These were very supple and nice to work. The leather was bought once or twice a year and when it arrived from Ipswich it was laid on shelves and big lumps of mutton fat, Russian tallow and grease were rubbed into it. We worked the fat in with a bone, just as a soldier bones his boots. Then we let it lay on the shelf for months and months before using it.

Our harness lasted for ever, as you might say. It was our downfall, wasn't it! We made these things so well that after a while they did us out of a living. We made plough collars for the Suffolk Punches and the great Percheron horses for 12s. 6d. each – fifteen bob if it was extra special. I made hundreds of these collars. Now it is almost impossible to buy one and if you could it would cost about £12. The price of a set of pony harness was five guineas. It was all marvellously hand-stitched with ten or twelve stitches to the inch and beautifully set out with a little iron.

You don't make much money if you work with your hands. You can't make the turnover. But I have no regrets working so slowly. I began in a world without time.

Looking back, I can see that the arrival of the village

bus was one of the first nails in the saddler's coffin. One farmer had a motor-plough, it is true, but he was rich. The bus told me that motors wouldn't always be for the rich. During the early part of the Great War some American tractors arrived – huge big things, nearly as vast as traction engines. We didn't worry too much because they couldn't be used in wet weather. When the farmers started buying self-binders I began to take an interest in canvas belts. Each binder would have three of these great belts and I learned how to repair them. After 1929 I concentrated on this canvas work, advertised and got most of the contracts for it in all the surrounding villages. It helped us over the change. Just after the last war the first Massey Harris combine arrived in Akenfield; but, again, it was one of those things you could only use on nice fine days. And you couldn't cut barley with it, only wheat. Now they are everywhere and the horses are quite gone.

My main job now is making big elevator canvasses for the pea-harvesting machines. I also make canvas covers for trollies on which to collect the game at shooting parties and halters for Tattersall's at Newmarket. I don't see that any craftsman has to stop; he has to develop.

Daphne Ellington · aged thirty-two · assistant teacher at Akenfield Primary School

I've lived in the country for a lot of my life but I've never felt that I belonged. I feel I want to spend only part of my life in a village, and particularly this village. It is so strange. Although I have lived in a number of country places and taught in three different village schools, I have never experienced such an atmosphere – in the school itself, I mean – as exists here. I don't know how to explain it, and I'm not really complaining *of* it. I have to talk about it simply because it is so curious. It is the power which the children have to resist everybody and everything outside the village.

At first I thought that the 11-plus selection had quite a lot to do with insularity. That the village children excluded newcomers like the children of American servicemen and of Ipswich business people who have bought houses in Akenfield because these pupils tend to get all the grammar school places. I mean, when you get seven successes and then you find that they are all imported pupils, it makes you think! But I've come to the conclusion that this strangeness I am trying to describe has nothing to do with this. The village children aren't jealous – on the contrary, they are convinced that they have something which none of the newcomers can ever have, some kind of mysterious life which is so perfect that it is a waste of time to search for anything else. I used to wonder at their slowness at absorbing things but now I am beginning to realize that they know from an early age that they don't need to take in what I am teaching them. They are dreadfully polite. They think that if they are polite it excuses everything. They will do anything you tell them but never that little extra original thing. They have solid faces which say, 'We will do what teacher wants us to do all day long, and then we'll do what *we* want to do!'

I have known instances of 'outside' children being beaten up or ridiculed but usually they are simply left on the perimeter of all the playground groups and when school is over, nobody walks home with them. There is just one game from which nobody is ever turned away. This is 'Peep-behind-the-curtain'. A child stands facing the wall while all the others creep up on him. Every now and then he turns round quickly and whoever he catches moving has to leave the game. It is the only game which everybody is allowed to play. The last person left among those creeping up takes the place of the child facing the wall. It is a game which is played with great intensity. The 'outside' child can win this game but it won't make any difference to his status. He will just have to go on watching when other games are played or, if he tries to join in, he will be ignored.

The school building is seventy-five years old and it was built on land given to Akenfield by a Victorian duke. It used to hold over ninety children but we don't have enough space with only forty-five. There are photographs of the old classes, with boys and girls packed together in tiers. They had to be absolutely still and absolutely silent, and absolutely obedient. Before the First World War, the farmers used to descend on a class now and then and demand the sons of their labourers to help them in the fields, and the teachers would let them go. Most of the parents and farmers thought that education simply interrupted work, and it is a bit like this still. The children are very involved with their parents' work and with adult gossip. Quite little boys will know the technical names of tractor attachments and what is going on in the fields at a particular time of the year and the girls talk together like grown women. Neither seem to want their childhood.

They are never imaginative because, again, they don't need to be. They find it impossible to want anything which they can't actually see in the village or which isn't theirs already. Adolescence makes them a bit restless, of course, but by then they are in such control of themselves that they rarely do anything unusual or exciting. They are very balanced but really it is only because they are so heavy! They never have any desire to explore an unknown area. They resist any pressure to make them inquisitive about things which lie beyond the scope of the village and should there be a boy or girl with initiative and a bright intelligence, he or she is soon frustrated. With most of them it is, 'We know quite enough for what we have to do, thank you very much.'

The mothers are only interested if their children can perform something, recite a poem by heart, strum a piece on the piano. They are proud then. They don't appreciate the need to ask why a thing is done. They say that they don't like their children to ask questions all the time; they think it is rude. There is something treasonable about a child who does well. A market gardener I know, who is now about twenty, is a lonely person because he went to the grammar school and the village women say, 'Didn't get him far, did it? All that schooling and he's still on the land!' Perhaps they know that there is nothing like education for breaking up an ordinary country family. Or perhaps theirs is a different wisdom.

The Cook's Tale

The dialect of the area has a gentle sing-song intonation which is allied with a pithy toughness. The following story, told before radio and other language-changing agencies arrived, gives some indication of the vigorous Suffolk speech and shows many old English words which are still in common use in the village. It also displays the somewhat laconic wit of the people. The story itself is Suffolk's claim – one of many – to the Rumpelstiltskin legend. It was told by a servant at the Big House many years ago.

*   *   *

TOM TIT TOT

Well, once upon a time there were a woman, and she baked five pies. And when they come out of the oven they was that overbaked, the crust were too hard to eat. So she says to her darter:

'Maw'r,' says she, 'put you them there pies on the shelf an' leave them a little, an' they'll come agin.' – She meant, you know, the crust 'ud get soft.

But the gal, she says to herself, 'Well, if they'll come agin, I'll ate 'em now.' And she set to work and ate 'em all, first and last.

Well, come supper time the woman she said: 'Goo you and git one o' them there pies. I dare say they've come agin now.'

The gal she went an' she looked, an' there warn't

nothin' but the dishes. So back she come, an' says she, 'Noo, they ain't come agin.'

'Not none o' them?' says the mother.

'Not none o' them,' says she.

'Well, come agin, or not come agin,' says the woman, 'I'll ha' one for supper.'

'But you can't if they ain't come,' says the gal.

'But I can,' says she. 'Goo you and bring the best of 'em.'

'Best or worst,' says the gal, 'I've ate 'em all, an' you can't ha' one till that's come agin.'

Well, the woman she were wholly bate, an' she took her spinnin' to the door to spin, and as she spun she sang:

'My darter ha' ate five, five pies to-day.
My darter ha' ate five, five pies to-day.'

The King, he were a' comin' down the street an' he hard her sing, but what she sang he couldn't hear, so he stopped and said,

'What were that you was a singin' of, maw'r?'

The woman, she were ashamed to let him hare what her darter had been a doin', so she sang, 'stids o' that:

'My darter ha' spun five, five skeins to-day.
My darter ha' spun five, five skeins to-day.'

'S'ars o' mine!' says the King, 'I never heerd tell o' anyone as could do that.'

Then he said: 'Look you here, I want a wife and I'll

marry your darter. But look you here,' says he, ' 'leven months out o' the year she shall have all the vittles she likes to eat, and all the gownds she likes to git, an' all the cump'ny she likes to hev; but the last month o' the year she'll ha' to spin five skeins ev'ry day, an' if she doon't, I shall kill her.'

'All right,' says the woman, for she thowt what a grand marriage there was. And as for them five skeins, when te come tew, there'd be plenty o' ways o' gettin' out of it, and likeliest, he'd ha' forgot about it.

Well, so they was married. An' for 'leven months the gal had all the vittles she liked to ate, and all the gownds she liked to git, and all the cump'ny she liked to hev. But when the time was over she began to think about them there skeins an' to wonder if he had 'em in mind. But not one word did he say about 'em, an' she whoolly thowt he'd forgot 'em.

Howsivir, the last day o' the last month, he takes her to a room she'd niver set eyes on afore. There worn't nothin' in it but a spinnin' wheel an' a stool. An', say he, 'Now me dear, hare you'll be shut in tomorrow with some vittles and some flax, and if you hain't spun five skeins by the night, yar hid'll goo off.'

An' away he went about his business. Well, she were that frightened. She'd allus been such a gatless mawther, that she didn't so much as know how to spin, an' what were she to dew tomorrer, with no one to come nigh to help her? She sat down on a stool in the kitchen, an' lork! how she did cry!

Howsivir, all on a sudden she hard a sort o' knockin' low down on the door. She upped and oped it, an' what should she see but a small little black thing with a long tail. That looked up at her right kewrious, an' that said:

'What are yew cryin' for?'

'What's that to yew?' says she.

'Nivir yew mind,' that said. 'But tell me what you're a cryin' for?'

'That oon't dew me noo good if I dew,' says she.

'You doon't know that,' that said, an' twirled that's tail round.

'Well,' says she, 'that oon't dew no harm, if that doon't dew no good,' and she upped an' she told about the pies an' the skeins an' everything.

'This is what I'll do,' says the little black thing. 'I'll come to yar winder iv'ry mornin' an' take the flax an' bring it spun at night.'

'What's your pay?' says she.

That looked out o' the corners o' that's eyes an' said: 'I'll give you three guesses every night to guess my name, an' if you hain't guessed it afore the month's up, yew shall be mine.'

Well, she thowt she'd be sure to guess that's name afore the month was up. 'All right,' says she, 'I agree.'

'All right,' says that, an' lork! how that twirled that's tail!

Well, the next day, har husband he took har into the room, an' there was the flax an' the day's vittles.

'Now there's the flax,' says he, 'an' if that ain't spun up this night off goo yar hid!' An' then he went out an' locked the door.

He'd hardly gone, when there was a knockin' agin the

winder. She upped and she oped it, an' there sure enough was the little oo'd thing a settin' on the ledge.

'Where's the flax?' says he.

'Here te be,' says she. And she gonned it to him.

Well, come the evenin', a knockin' come agin to the winder. She upped and she oped it and there was the little oo'd thing with five skeins of flax on his arm.

'Here to be,' says he, and he gonned it to her. 'Now what's my name?' says he.

'What, is that Bill?' says she.

'Noo, that ain't,' says he. An' he twirled his tail.

'Well, is that Ned?' says she.

'Noo, that ain't,' says he. An' he twirled his tail.

'Well, is that Mark?' says she.

'Noo, that ain't,' says he. And he twirled harder, an' awa' he flew.

Well, har husband he come in, there was the five skeins riddy for him. 'I see I shan't hev for to kill you to-night, me dare,' says he. 'Yew'll hev yar vittles and yar flax in the mornin',' says he, an' awa' he goes.

Well, ivery day the flax and the vittles, they was brought, an' ivery day that there little black impet used to come mornins and evenins. An' all the day the mawther she set a tryin' fur to think o' names to say to it when te come at night. But she niver hit on the right one. An' as that got to-warts the ind o' the month, the impet that began to look soo maliceful, an' that twirled that's tail faster an' faster each time she gave a guess.

At last te come to the last day but one. The impet that come along o' the five skeins an' that said:

'What, hain't yew got my name yet?'

'Is that Nicodemus?' says she.

'Noo, t'ain't,' that says.

'Is that Sammle?' says she.

'Noo, t'ain't,' that says.

'A-well, is that Methusalem?' says she.

'Noo, t'ain't that norther,' he says.

Then that looks at her with that's eyes like a cool o'fire, an' that says: 'Woman, there's only tomorrer night, and then yar'll be mine!' An' away that flew.

Well, she felt that horrud. Howsomediver, she hard the King a comin' along the passage. In he came, an' when he see the five skeins, he says, says he:

'Well, my dare,' says he, 'I don't see but what you'll ha' your skeins riddy tomorrer night as well, an' as I reckon I shan't ha' to kill you, I'll ha' supper in here tonight.' So they brought supper, an' another stool for him, and down the tew they set.

Well, he hadn't eat but a mouthful or so, when he stops an' begins to laugh.

'What is it?' says she.

'A-why,' says he, 'I was out a huntin' to-day, an' I got awa' to a place in the wood I'd never seen afore. An' there was an' ol' chalk pit. An' I heerd a sort o' a hummin', kind o'. So I got off my hobby, and went right quiet to the pit, an' I looked down. Well, what should be there but the funniest little black thing yew iver set eyes on. An' what was that dewin' on, but that had a little spinnin' wheel, an' that were spinnin' wonnerful fast, an' twirlin' that's tail. An' as that span that sang:

'Nimmy nimmy not
My name's Tom Tit Tot.'

Well, when the mawther heerd this, she fared as if she could ha' jumped outer her skin for joy, but she didn't say a word.

Next day, that there little thing looked soo maliceful when he come for the flax. An' when night come, she heerd that a knockin' agin the winder panes. She oped the winder, an' that came right in on the ledge. That were grinnin' from are to are, an' Oo! that's tail were twirlin' round that fast!

'What's my name?' that says, as that gonned har the skeins.

'Is that Solomon?' she says, pretendin' to be afeared.

'Noo, t'aint,' that says, an' that come fudder into the room.

'Well, is that Zebedee?' says she again.

'Noo, t'ain't,' says the impet. An' then that laughed an' twirled that's tail till yew cou'n't hardly see it.

'Take time, woman,' that says; 'next guess an' you'll be mine.' An' that stretched out that's black hands at her.

Well, she backed a step or two, an' she looked at it, and then she laughed out, and says she, a pointin' of her finger at it,

'Nimmy nimmy not,
Yar name's Tom Tit Tot!'

Well, when that hard her, that shruck awful, an' awa' that flew into the dark, an' she niver saw it noo more.

Alan Mitton · aged thirty-eight · orchard foreman

I am an orchard man. The orchards I was born into, as you might say, are the biggest in the village. There are nearly 140 acres of them and they lie on the slopes to the south of the houses. More people are employed here than anywhere else in the village. I actually started work on this farm three years before I left school, mostly during the summer holidays. And then, when I left school, the farmer said, 'You used to enjoy being on the fruit cart, maybe you would like to stay on it regular?' I said, 'I would rather', and that is how I came to be in the fruit all the while.

When they first planted the orchards, before the First War, they began with just a little patch containing two or three trees of each kind of fruit and then they began to lay out the Bramley orchards – probably about five acres apiece. And gradually the orchards spread their way up the hill – because of frost reasons, I suppose. We've got about nine acres of old-established Bramleys left from those days. Some are over fifty years old and if the pruning is done correctly there is no reason why these trees shouldn't go on for always. Right at the bottom of this old orchard there is a row of the original trees planted in the 1890s – just five trees planted at twelve yards square, which is double the space usually given to a Bramley. One of these five trees, which is nearly eighty years old, never produces less than twenty bushels of apples. And the funny thing is that the apples are all big. No one really knows why this tree is so marvellous, why every year without fail, as you might say, it gives eighteen out of its twenty bushels which are first-class apples. In 1965, which was a good apple year, we picked 124 bushels of fruit off this one row of old trees. The next row, where the trees have only half the space, gave 120 bushels.

In the days when I began, out of the twenty men on the fruit farm, only four were allowed to prune. This was because of the old-fashioned idea that when you were cutting a piece of wood you were taking so many apples off the tree. So the trees went up and up, and bushed out and became enormous. They got so thick that it was difficult to spray them and so tall it was hard to gather. And they didn't get enough air. But about fifteen years ago we tried a new drastic cutting method. We said, 'Right! We'll have this bit out and this bit out!' The old men came and looked and said, 'You aren't pruning, you're pollarding!' They were very shocked. 'Poor trees, poor trees . . .' they said. All the middles were ripped out; the trees looked like umbrellas. In fact, it looked really shameful. It was always the old boys' pride to keep the shape of a tree, so they were shocked. It was their main art, to keep the tree-shape. Well, nothing was said. The sawing went on. The middles were taken right out and the lower boughs removed so that the tractors and sprayers could drive through the orchard. These trees looked terrible and the next year they grew so much spur-wood where the boughs had been that we wondered if we had done right. Then, the *next* year, the fruit started to come. It was exciting. The apples got better and better. It was amazing; you had to see it to believe it.

So much changed after this. Once, you had to wait five years between planting a tree and picking its fruit, now it is only three. These young trees are no more than three feet high and with a stick no rounder than your thumb. They have had their tops cut off at knee level and have burst out into four or five branches which, a year or so later, have been cut halfway back again – tipping, we call it – and then the third year we have the apples. You can pick as many as twenty pounds of apples from a fourth-year tree. It is all so quick.

We buy our trees from a nursery in Sussex. They come as maidens, which is a first-year tree which has been grafted and budded. We plant them at the end of the year and then, just before the sap rises, we snip the top out. Should any flowering buds appear the first year, we rub them off. We never let apples come the first year. These trees are low and small, so that we can pick the fruit easily. All the big trees are gradually disappearing.

We are expanding the Coxes. Twenty years ago there wasn't a Cox tree on the farm at all. We were told that the soil in the village was wrong for Coxes and that they wouldn't grow. The only field which might grow them, they said, was down by the river. They said they might grow there. But then, they said, the frost will lie in the river belt, so better not plant there. Well, we planted them on the slope with a pollinater and they have borne extremely heavy. Coxes are expensive apples but very popular; there is always a sale for them. You can eat them all the way through from early October to February and they will always be good, whereas an apple like a Worcester can only be eaten in September for the full flavour. It soon goes clung, as we say. We pollinate the Coxes with James Grieves – one James Grieve to about every fifteen Coxes. If it looks like an apple-glut year and we think that the Grieves aren't going to sell very well, we pick the biggest of them in early September and sell them as cookers. The apples which are left on the James Grieve trees won't be picked at all. They will just drop onto the ground. Last year they were all picked and sold because the spring frosts caused an apple shortage.

We're growing Matsus, which is a new kind of apple from Japan which has been crossed with a Golden Delicious. There are more Golden Delicious apples grown in the world than any other variety. We find that the Matsu will hang on the tree longer than any other apple. With Coxes, you've got to rush and pick before the mid-October winds take them off but there is no hurry with a Matsu. It will hang firm until you have finished picking all your main eaters and cookers. Last year, this one particular Matsu which we grew on trial had eleven apples on it. They were great things. We cut one up into pieces for the women to try and they said it was juicy and nice and fine-flavoured. This year, this same tree bore 511 pounds of fruit! The weight of it carried the boughs to the grass, so that it was like an open parasol. Every apple went over the two-inch mark, which is the grade an apple has to be for market. So we are pleased with the Matsus.

Like everything else in the village, the fruit trees are being made to fit into less and less space. We have four acres of apples which Mike Poole and myself trim on the 'pillar' system, pruning away so that a maiden is left with the main stem going up to about ten feet eventually. It is a bit complicated to learn. It means that instead of getting 132–6 trees on an acre of land, you can get over 300. It also means that all the apples are low enough to be picked from a short pair of steps. But we have come up against a snag. With so much pruning you get a lot of little spurs and a density of leaves, so the apples don't ripen all that well.

Michael Poole · aged thirty-seven · orchard worker

I used to get up of a morning. I used to take two pails. I used to climb Scarlett Hill to the pump. I used to carry the water home. I used to find the house all dark, all sleeping. I used to clank the pails and shout, 'Come you together now! Let's be having you!' and my dad would jump out of bed *bang!* I used to walk back to Scarlett Hill, to old Mackay's house. I used to hang around his door and then go in and watch him cut fat bacon and slip it in the pan. Then eggs. I used to say, 'Is that your breakfast then, Mr Mackay?' and he'd say, 'That is.' He'd slip a bit more into the pan – 'For the dog,' he'd say. 'What dog, Mr Mackay?' – 'That damn young puppy,' he'd say. I used to take a chair. After breakfast I used to say, 'It's nice for you to have a mite of company like, Mr Mackay.' And he'd say, 'Oh?' I used to be ten then.

I went to work on the fruit when I was fourteen. I never minded it. I got my money and that was the main thing. I grew, my money grew. It was nice to have it.

Summer was best. You'd get the women come and

give you a look. You'd torment them and they'd torment you. There used to be a regular procession of old girls who'd bike up from Framlingham for the picking. When I was sixteen, one of these old girls came up to me in the orchard and said, 'Let me see your watch.'

I didn't answer.

'Aren't you going to let me see your watch then?'

I said nothing. Anyway, she could see my watch; it was lying on my waistcoat under the apple tree.

'I shall take it . . .' she says.

'Take it then.'

'I reckon you want me to take it?'

'I can see you're bent on it,' I said, 'so you may as well.'

So she took it, for devilry. It was on a chain and she hung it round her fat neck the whole live-long afternoon. I wouldn't let her see it worried me. She'd walk by and shout, 'Come and get it!'

I said nothing. She brought it to me about five, before she set off home. She put it over my head like a necklace and said, 'There you are, you young bugger.'

I wouldn't speak to her.

The next morning, along she comes, straight to where I'm about to start. Her arms were stuck out full length and she was all smiles. She got her mouth on my face and, my God, she must have thought it was her breakfast, or something.

I pushed at her. I said, 'Don't! Look out, he's coming!' – He was, too. Old Fletcher the foreman. She broke away but back she arrived later when I was lying on the scythings, eating my bait. It was long grass all around.

'Don't fret,' says she.

I said nothing.

'The coast is clear,' she says, and comes down on me like a ton of bricks. I couldn't see nothing but grass. There was such a rocking. I couldn't tell whether I was babe or man.

At tea-time the women went rushing home with their aprons full of apples – shrieking, you can be sure. They shruck a bit more when they saw me and a couple of them rang their bike bells. My old woman shouted, 'Don't torment him! He's like his old watch – not so bad when he's wound up!' Laugh! You should have heard them!

It was my first time.

Christ, that was a summer and no mistake.

Marjorie Jope · aged seventy-nine · retired District Nurse

I started in 1925 with Akenfield and three other villages and then, in two–three months, some more villages came under my care until I had nine altogether. I was a novelty, I can tell you. None of these places had had a nurse before; the births and deaths were attended by secretive old women, just as in the olden days. I was appointed by the local nursing association which was affiliated to the East Suffolk Nursing Association. I had a little car. There were no cars then, so you can imagine how important I looked! My salary was £2 a week and at first my father had to help me pay my lodgings. I had to pay all my own expenses but soon the villages had to raise my salary. This was done by individual people paying the Nursing Association 4s. a year. Well-off people paid more. My first lodgings were with an old lady who disapproved if I went out earlier than nine in the morning or got back later than four in the afternoon. I changed lodgings a few times because nobody understood that I had to be free to go out and come in at all hours. The vicar had to be severe with them. His name was Mr Paternoster and the verger's name was Creed. It sounds funny but it was a fact. Anyway, the vicar said, 'We've got a nurse now and we're not going to let her go', and then he searched around and eventually found me a kind of hut. I soon made it into a house and then I was independent. The relief! I paid rent for it and I was always on duty in it, although officially I had Thursday afternoons off. I had the telephone and that was a novelty too. Most ordinary people didn't use the phone: they walked or biked miles and miles with news of accidents, maternity cases, troubles of all sorts. What with the phone and people calling at all hours, it was non-stop. I often wonder how I did it. But I was young and the young find all things possible.

There was a great difference inside the cottages in those days. One had to explain every single thing. The most simple instructions had to be said twice over. Living conditions were very, very poor. Akenfield was an agricultural labourers' village. The only 'people' here were the Cretinghams. They were the only 'people', you understand. So everything fell on me. I was school nurse, too, and once or twice a year, when the school doctor came round, I had to assist him examine the children. I knew them all so well they could have been my own children. I knew their homes and in most cases I had delivered them. There were so many dirty children in those days, dirty hair, dirty feet, impetigo. It was thought a disgrace to have a dirty head, but lots did. There's nothing like that now. Children have never been as beautiful as they are now. There were quite a lot of 'home' children in the village in those days – more than twenty, perhaps. They came from Dr Barnardo's and from the Church of England Children's Home. They were all boys – nobody wanted girls. They came sometimes when they were only a few weeks' old but they were rarely adopted in the full legal sense, perhaps because the foster-parents would lose the home-allowance if they were. Two of these boys became a schoolmaster and a Battle of Britain pilot and both tried to find out who they really were, but they never did. A lot of the Barnardo boys were sent to Australia when they were fourteen and new ones came in their place. Their foster-parents didn't seem to turn a hair when the replacement happened; it always amazed me.

The old people were not taken care of. This is another thing which people like to think now, that grandfathers and grandmothers had an honoured place in the cottage. In fact, when they got old they were just neglected, pushed away into corners. I even found them in cupboards! Even in fairly clean and respectable houses you often found an old man or woman shoved out of sight in a dark niche. People were most suspicious at first when I called. There was no such thing as a welcome, you had to make your own way. They didn't want anybody outside to know their business. I had to ask questions, especially about TB. They hated that. I had to collect long lists of facts about them and they were so unwilling that it often took me days. I had to feel my way, exchanging trust for trust. They had their secrets, like all families, but I had to know some of them! There were families in Akenfield who never told anyone anything. It was – their entire life, you know – all bolted up behind the back door. Not many people were taken away to the infirmaries. They were born at home and they died at home. I now know so much about them all – things nobody else could ever know. In time I heard everything. They told me things they could not tell each other. I knew them body and mind. None of them, neither the best nor the worst, were so very different to each other, if they did but know it. They liked to imagine they were, of course. I suppose we all do. Five years after I arrived in Akenfield it got so that I could walk in nearly every house. Sometimes they all looked so strong and well that I wondered why I had been sent for, then the worry would come spilling out. It was usually about the relations. Practically every family was related. It is the same with myself, except I don't know my own cousins. So many village marriages used to be cousin marriages. It is different now because the young men drive about all over the place and find girls. Nobody moved a yard in the old days.

People died from much the same things as they do now, except there was more cancer then, unless they whip the cancer patients off to Ipswich and one doesn't hear of it. If they thought they had cancer in the old days they would keep quiet about it. They put up with it in secret for as long as they could. Things were more or less hidden – all life was hidden – and then, of course, it was difficult to move the doctors. They didn't bother too much. Time after time I would try and get a doctor to a bad case in the village but most times he never came. He would come when he thought he would. Sick people were on parish relief but the doctors ran their own medical clubs. If people didn't pay into the club, then they didn't get a doctor. A doctor could not be reported for not coming, although I did report a doctor once. It was for refusing to believe that a woman had TB and telling her to get up. She got up and she collapsed. But then there was Dr Denny who would come out any time of the day or night. He was most unusual. There were quite a few country doctors in the neighbourhood but none of them did this. They were important folk then and the villagers were a bit nervous of them. But Dr Denny was different. Even if it was somebody else's case, he'd come. As for the old family doctor – he was for the old families, if you know what I mean.

People think of me as the person who is present at the beginning of their lives but in most cases I have been present at the end of them too. I used to stay up one night or several nights when they were passing. Some talked of God, but very, very few. Even the people who had been brought up in chapel or church rarely talked of God as they died. It is a fact. What can you make of it? I was with them as they passed. Not much talk of God at the last.

Quite a lot of old people spent their last weeks alone. Their absence of family was only noticed at this time. I remember a clean, respectable old man who lived in a hut on the Framlingham Road. His name was Dixon and the name of his hut was 'Travel On'. He had not worked in Akenfield but had arrived there, presumably after he had retired. Some people said he had been a sailor. He certainly looked clean like a sailor. Then people began to say, where was he? Where had he got to? So the vicar went to 'Travel On' and, oh dear! What a sight. Apparently Mr Dixon had been terribly ill and had just laid in his hut. Worse, he had tried to light his oil-stove to keep warm and had knocked it over and burnt himself. The vicar had walked up after midday Communion on Sunday, just to say hello, as he thought. Instead of which he spent all the afternoon cleaning Mr Dixon and scrubbing 'Travel On' out. He was so convinced that it was a case of village neglect that he prayed about it during the evening service, but we later discovered that Mr Dixon had been attended by his own doctor, who, seeing he couldn't last much longer, had simply shut the door on him. There were plenty of things like that. I often found awful, dreadful things. The village wasn't shocked. They expected people 'to go a bit behind at the end'.

I'm making it sound miserable, aren't I? It wasn't really. It is just that Akenfield is still very close to the old conditions. People weren't worried about these conditions because they were the only ones they knew. They were natural but bad. There was no main water. We all drank from the ponds or the pump or from some wells. It was nothing for me to nurse where the boiled water was bright green! As for my equipment, well I will tell you. I had a saucepan for boiling up my instruments, a spirit stove and several enamel bowls. I carried all this stuff about from house to house in a huge American cloth bag which I made myself. I used to have to strain all the village water through muslin before I dared use it. As well as these things, I carried plenty of odd pieces of mackintosh and a big bundle of clean rags – torn sheets from the better-off houses mostly. We never had nearly enough dressings. As for drugs, well there was aspirin and little else. People in great pain might be given occasional morphia by the doctor. Nothing much. On the whole, people took pain and illness for granted; they weren't very frightened. They didn't worry very much. They supposed they would get better. Nor did they seem fearful of death. They had all worked so hard and so long, I suppose there was a kind of comfort in it.

Mothers worried most. Families were so big that there was nothing restful in lying upstairs with a house full of children. Some families, well you knew that they did not have enough to eat, but they wouldn't tell you. Nor could you find out. Not the real facts. I had a case on the Myddleton Road – a young mother – I knew perfectly well what the trouble was. She was hungry. So I saw the vicar and he got some of the church charity money, which was lying in the bank from one year to the next, and we bought her some ordinary good food. That was all the medicine she needed. We always tried to get the mothers to come to the village school when the county council doctor examined the children, but when he asked them what they gave these thin boys to eat the answer was always, 'porridge, eggs, meat, cake . . .' You should have heard! All the mothers thought it right to lie. They thought it shameful not to be able to feed their children, not to be able to manage. Yet I knew of quite a few children who came to school without any breakfast and who walked home to dinner after dinner of just potatoes. That was what they ate, potatoes, and for tea, bread and jam. They had meat on Sunday. And suet puddings and jam. It was easier for the children when they were babies for then they came under what we called 'infant life protection visits' and a very good committee which saw that they had food and clothes. There was little or no cruelty where children were concerned. The stick was used but it was thought quite normal and nobody took much notice of such punishments, although there was talk about a man in the next village who used to whip his daughters. They were getting big girls and they would walk freely along the roads.

Did you know about our gipsies? They came every November to winter down by the Drift on the lower road. They used to camp there in what I called igloos – half hooped tents. The village didn't like them a bit, but in those days they didn't like anyone except themselves. They were always hostile, always suspicious. It is so different now. Looking back, I see this hostility as the worst thing. The least question and they froze. Eventually I found out that I had to get my answers without asking questions. The gipsies were so used to cold faces that they took them for granted. They had lots of babies but in all my nursing years I was only asked to visit them once, and then it was a false alarm. The young father had heated up the water on a tripod and the mother was lying in a glittering, spotless caravan. What a difference to the cottages! An old gipsy, Mr Martin, died in his caravan and it was burnt on the day of his funeral. This was in 1936. He had several children including a girl named Ocean who was a famous Suffolk pedlar – cottons, buttons, things like that. All Ocean's children are married and live in houses now. There are eighteen people in Akenfield who are descended from the Drift gipsies. They are the good-looking ones – you can't miss them.

The village people tend not to look old when they are no longer very young. It is hard to tell their age above fifty. They are strong, quiet people. They endure. Some cannot, of course. There was this middle-aged farmer at Plomesgate, well to see him you wouldn't think he had a care in the world above a bit of a bad leg – nothing to worry about really. Then came this message to say, 'come quick'. It's his leg, I thought. When I arrived, there was his wife and all the neighbours huddled like hens in the parlour. A woman said, 'He's through there, nurse.' So I went into a shed, with her following, but when I started to pick up a sack she cried, 'Oh, don't do that while I'm here. Don't! Don't!' The farmer had slashed his throat in the shed. That morning he had got up and made the tea as usual. Then he took some up to his wife and drank some himself, then he strolled up to the shed with his razor . . . He had almost cut his head off. 'Bind that up, nurse,' said the doctor when he arrived. That nearly finished me for laying-out. I had to put it in my report, you see, and except for mothers and children it was against the rules to lay-out bodies. All the same, I did it and I went on doing it after I retired. When people want help they must have it. What matters more than this? I wash and straighten them for the grave. It is such a small thing and somebody must do it for *me*. It is such a small thing but people cannot bring themselves to do it. They find it hard to think away from themselves. It is sometimes why they are as they are. They are learning all the time.

Bruce Buckley · *aged seventeen* · *forge apprentice*
Thomas Dix · *aged seventeen* · *farm worker*

Bruce and Thomas (Tompo) are the classic mates of the 'Til-death-do-us-part' kind and are at present at the zenith of the bosom-pal stage. Time, with its steadying proprieties, is the only thing which will prevent them colliding joyously like a couple of ponies whenever they meet. Mrs Sullivan pushed them into the same double desk on their first day at school when they were five and told them to look after each other. An arranged mateship which works has followed. At eleven, they were both pulled out of a hole in the ice, drowned to all accounts. At thirteen they ran away to hitch-hike. Where? That was the problem. So after two days of it they walked home. These two events seem to have made them staid, cautious and quite gratuitously contented.

Bruce is thin and fair. His long, pale neck grows out of his leather jacket like an iris stylosa stem out of glossy damp, dark mould. He is watchful, sharp. He thinks quite a bit of himself but his friend manages to rub the edge off the worst of Bruce's conceit without his realizing it. Tompo, in fact, makes Bruce more likeable than he would be if left on his own.

Tompo himself is square and dark, with a ready-to-smile furry, red-brown face and an expansive, roly-poly body. A plain, good-natured Morland character. Both boys giggle a lot and exude a challenging kind of mindless delight. They have an occasional way of tumbling over each other like cubs which seems to irritate older people, who frown. Both have established reputations for accomplishing prodigious amounts of work. They chat cheerfully across each other in an amiably disconnected sort of way. Their world is small and they are determined to keep it so.

TOMPO: What do we do? We read books. . . .

BRUCE: I don't have much time so I read small books . . .

TOMPO: We've been to Woodbridge this afternoon, just to walk round, and that. We're going to the pictures in Ipswich tonight. We're going to see a film called *Casino Royale*. We only go to the pictures in the winter; in the summer we like to get our motor-bikes out and zoom around. We go into all the other villages and drink Coke and shandy in their pubs. We don't look at things much. I like to see the birds but I can't say that I'm very interested in them. Let them fly about, I say. Suffolk is a great place for birds. Everybody knows this.

BRUCE: Last night I went brushing for Colonel Eldon. They got 210 pheasants. I'm not a good shot myself, I tend to miss everything. The Colonel rears about 600 birds and holds four shoots a year. Yesterday, there were eight guns and fifteen brushers. I like to meet the guns and brush for them because they pay me pretty well. I get 36s., a bottle of beer and a packet of cigs. I like birds too.

TOMPO: We've been friends for years and years and years.

BRUCE: I earn £6 flat. This is what I take. Motor mechanic boys would be lucky to get £3 4s.

TOMPO: Sometimes, when my mates have been with me chopping out sugar-beet, I've made as much as £15 clear. This is on piece-work, mind you. But my usual wage without deductions is £5 14s. 6d. I stick it into my wallet, you know. When I was young I put it in the bank. Now I keep it in my wallet in case I need to spend it. It is nice to have money. I bought this motor-bike six months ago.

BRUCE: Girls take your money – Tompo's had nine girls.

TOMPO: Well, not *had* them . . .

BRUCE: You *had* one of them –

TOMPO: He gets a bonus on top of his wages – £4 5s. a month. It's a share-out of the profits which the forge makes every month. They must be doing pretty well if they can afford to give that much back.

BRUCE: There's a girl in Saxmundham who would be easy for Tompo but he won't look at her.

TOMPO: Who's talking about girls?

BRUCE: It's all right for you. (Pause) I didn't have to apply for the job at the forge, you know – *they* asked *me*. I'm glad that they did.

TOMPO: I started going to the Agricultural Training Centre last September. The term starts in September and ends in March, so that we have six months off during the busy time on the farm. I am doing a three-year course because I am an apprentice but some farm boys only go for two years. I work for the farmer who hires land from my father, so I am really working my father's farm for another man. I am particularly interested in farm machinery. We have 600 acres and two tractors, and we mostly grow spring barley. Then it will be winter wheat. We have forty acres of sugar-beet and 100 acres of peas for Birdseye.

BRUCE: I once found an old, old book dated 1874. It was full of recipes to cure horses and oxen. It had a cure for foot-and-mouth disease. The master read it and said, 'Rubbish'. My father, who was a horseman, read it and said nothing.

TOMPO: When I was a little boy I used to come outside and watch the horses on the farm. There were six, then there were five, then there were none. I didn't care. I'd sooner have a tractor any day. This is just my opinion, you understand. They just stick you on a tractor now and say, 'plough the field up'. Easy! You stick your old wheel down and – plough! Who worries if it isn't straight?

BRUCE: Arnie.

TOMPO: Oh, Arnie! Bugger Arnie. (Mimicking) 'When I was your age, I didn't get five or six quid a week, I got five or six bob!' Arnie's old. He's fifty-four.

BRUCE: We shall be fifty-four one day – *in the same month*.

TOMPO: Well, let's hope we both live to see it. We're learning Old Time Dancing at the youth club; that should come in handy. It is a very big club and people come to it from miles around on their bikes. They are nearly all village boys.

BRUCE: And girls.

TOMPO: And girls. Saturday night is the village night out. In the summer we all zoom off to Felixstowe on our bikes. We don't swim there. We swim in the river at Melton. Did you know that there are a tidy few swimming pools in the gardens round here? The farmers built them – I don't know why because they can't swim. We go to Wimbledon to watch the stock-car racing. I used to be mechanic to a stock-car driver. We also go to the wrestling at Felixstowe. It looks pretty terrible but it isn't really. It is all put on. Anyway, the men don't wrestle well if they're not being televised, and you can't blame them. What do we like doing best of all? – motor-bike scrambling. This is the most favourite thing in the whole village. We all belong to a motor-bike club – there are more than fifty of us – and we all go off to the scrambles at Blaxhall and Wakes Colne. The club costs us 10s. a year and we meet every Tuesday night. Our leather clothes are expensive but they keep us warm. We have ordinary haircuts, as you can see. Maybe mine is fairly long. It is just to keep my head warm. When it begins to blow in the wind, then I begin to think about the barber. There's some very fancy dressing now, isn't there? People who want to do it should do it. Why not?

BRUCE: Have you seen Hughie?

TOMPO: Hughie's O.K.

BRUCE: I didn't say he wasn't, did I?

TOMPO: You're a nut.

BRUCE: (Amazed) *I* am?

TOMPO: (of Bruce) What would you do with him? – you tell me. [Uproar. Tina, a sheepdog, joins in. Bruce's mother rushes in.] 'Clear out you together now! Whenever are you going to grow up? Grow up, do!'

Anthony Summer · aged twenty-three · shepherd

I was born in Akenfield. All my family is here, my
mother, my uncles, my aunties and my granny. But not
my father – he was a sailor and was drowned when I
was a baby. The ship he was on was torpedoed during
the last war as it was sailing through the Dodecanese
Islands and he has no grave. When the Greeks put up a
memorial to all the British men who were killed helping
them, the Legion paid my mother's and my fares to see
the unveiling. I was sixteen. The princesses of Greece
shook my hand and I walked through Athens. Greece is
a very nice place. I think about it. You get such contrasts
there. I would like to go back to it. There are no middle
people, as in Suffolk, only rich and poor. We drank goat's
milk there – just as we have always done at home. I was
pleased to see the Greeks drinking goat's milk because it
is free from bruc and very good for asthma. I also drank
ouzo and ate honey, and sometimes I thought how
strange it was that I was walking about in Athens because
my father was in the Greek sea.

This was the year I went to Chadacre Agricultural
College, which is one of the oldest of the agricultural
training places. I had done a year on a farm before going
there. It was just a job at first and then I began to like it.
My mother said, 'If you're going farm-working, you're
going to do it properly. You are going to be a trained
man – so no arguing.' So I applied and was accepted.
There were about fifty students there and they mostly

came from Suffolk, Norfolk and Essex. Nobody special-
ized in anything: we each took the general course of
management, sheep, cows and machinery. The College
has changed a lot since it was founded and most of
the boys who go there are much better educated than
they were before the war. They are nearly all farmers'
sons or village boys like myself – hardly anybody from
a town.

There were only a few sheep on the farm when I
started here at fifteen, then, when I got back from being
trained at the college, the farmer took on some more
and we had about 250 all told. We did so well out of
these that we lost our heads and went straight up to
1,000! Then the profit margin dropped and we soon cut
back to 500. This was a good number; it meant that I
could look after all of them myself – plus William.
William is my dog. He was bought by the farm but he
thinks he is my dog, and I think he is too. He does a
good half of the work. He can do anything. He can put
the whole flock through the footbath without my even
being in the field, and he is fond of conversation.

The autumn is the beginning of the shepherd's year,
as you might say. The tups go into the ewes about the
first week in September. These aren't the proper tups;
they just bring the ewes on. We call them teasers. It
means that when you put in the proper tups the ewes
are good and ready for them, and can be served in one
bunch. Let them love together and they'll lamb together,
and that will be convenient. A good ram will serve fifty
ewes after the teasers have been with them for a month.

I work it like this. I put half my proper tups in with the ewes for two days, then take them out and give them a rest while the other half have a go. Each ram has a harness full of crayon strapped round him, so that when he jumps he marks the ewe. I then know how many ewes are coming. I change the crayon – the raddle – every fifteen days. So the first raddle will be blue, then red. In the olden days they painted the jumped ewes with red ochre but now we have this system of telling. If all the ewes are covered the first fifteen days and none of them come back, then I take the tups out. I leave them roughly three periods to come over – about forty-five days all told.

I usually start lambing in mid-February, although one year I started as early as Christmas Day. It was much too soon. The grass wasn't ready so the lambs had to be kept indoors. The food bills were terrific! I don't have to help a great deal with the births, only be there. This is most important. I never leave the flock then, I am there all the time. I only call the vet if there is a big mishap, such as the womb coming out. I take each lamb away from its mother and do all the little odds and ends like. You can't raise every lamb which is born, there must be some loss. I try and arrange things so that each ewe has two lambs. This shouldn't be difficult if each ewe has been well flushed before the tup services her and has had good pasture. You see, before tupping time the ewes are kept on a bare pasture and then, just a week before the rams are put in, I put them on a high plane of nutrition which is supposed to bring down more ovaries. And so two eggs will come down, and I have had three and even four. I had five sets of quads last year but they were poor little runty things.

I castrate the male lambs, the little tups, about an hour after they have been born. They say that what you've never had, you never miss. I wonder. I do it with rubber rings. It used to be done much later. The tails used to be cut off with a hot iron and the balls nicked out with the shepherd's teeth. He ate well that day. But the tups still go behind a bit after they have been castrated. They get thin. It pulls them down. It is a surprising thing to happen to you when you have just come into the world on a spring morning. And, of course, I cut the tails off later on – to prevent fly-strike in the summer-time.

I like to sell the first crop of lambs at about twelve or thirteen weeks old when they weigh about seventy-five pounds. There would be about thirty-five lambs in this crop. Some go to the local market and some to the meat-traders – British Beef. The late lambs are sold about September and a few are carried over the winter and not sold until the following spring. But I haven't got enough grass to keep the store lambs through the winter.

I did my first shearing this summer. I sheared 500 ewes. The wife came out and rolled the wool for me and it took us just under the week – that was everything. We took the ewes out from the lambs about seven in the morning and worked right through until about nine at night. We worked every hour that was possible. I used electric shears and now and then I gave some poor old sheep a nip, but nothing as bad as would have happened had I been using the old-fashioned shears. The year [1967] was better than average for the price of wool.

Nobody tries to keep a really big sheep farm in East Anglia these days. Sheep are fitted in with the crop rotations and are just part of the farm. My sheep are put on to rye grass and they also have hay and pea silage, carrot wastage, etc. The ewes also get two pounds of concentrates each when they lamb in order to prevent pregnancy toxaemia. But they get things wrong with them, bad feet mostly. Foot-rot and flies, these are the bad things with sheep. I put them through a footbath twice a week. There is very little intensive sheep-farming in the villages round here although I hear that somebody is trying it out near Diss. He has his sheep on slats, like calves. Poor sheep! that is what I say. I bring my sheep in during the winter but they're out in the air all the rest of the year.

I sometimes think of shepherding in a big way – all young shepherds do. Here we buy-in old ewes and sell them out for meat. But I quite like the idea of breeding and selling pedigree animals. And I'd like to show. This farm only shows in the lamb carcass competitions which means that you show three sheep, then one is picked out, killed and its carcass is judged. I'd sooner show live. My best friend is a Dorset shepherd and he's got a pedigree flock to show down there. I envy him rather.

I belong to Suffolk but I wouldn't mind moving. I once even thought of going to Australia but then I thought to myself, 'Supposing you get out there and you don't like it – then what will you do?' You need a lot of money to start in Australia. All the same, it is always in the back of my mind to do a bit of farming on my own. I'd like to own something, even if it is only a little smallholding where I can keep pigs. Being on my own is a dream which I want to come true. I don't want to get old and look back and think that I have been looking after somebody else's sheep all my life. But land is dear here – too dear. So I don't know what will happen.

It is easy on the farms against what it used to be. The old men wore their bodies to death but we only wear out a few machines. We all get on very well together on the farm. Ages don't count. There is an old shepherd who still works here part-time and he has helped me a lot. He lends me books and tells me many things. The young men are very fond of him because he is so interesting. It is pleasant here but, all the same, I dream, I make plans. I think you must have some ambition – not just carry on. I mustn't get old and look back at nothing. If you can look back on a farm which you have built up, that is something. If you haven't struggled to do something different – better – by the time you are thirty it is all up with you.

[. . .]

Derek Warren · aged twenty-nine · ploughman

I have been ploughing continuously since last June. All the time. Now it is February and I haven't stopped. I have ploughed every day, Sundays too, for eight months. But it is nearly finished now. There will be a break until after the harvest, then, as soon as a field is cleared, I'll be on it. There are about 400 acres of corn-land and I plough it all. All the fields are different. They have their names and they feel to be different places. It is how it should be. I wouldn't like the village to become a Tannington where the hedges have gone and the plough-man doesn't know where he is. A well-kept hedge is a good sight and tells you where you are. The hedges belong to the village. You get so used to seeing them standing there – they are like buildings and you miss them when they are knocked down. Some hedges are important and when they go you feel as bad as if a wood had been taken away. I think that there are certain hedges which the farmers shouldn't touch without asking the people – although I can't see this happening.

I'm contented here. I haven't got the education for a farm manager's job and I wouldn't like it even if I had. All the same, as things are today you really do want some education whatever you do. But if you haven't got it you must learn contentment. Without education you can pick up plenty of practical experience on the farm, but you'll never grasp the new theory or understand the money. If I had gone to the agricultural college it would all have been different, no doubt. I started off working with the cows when I first left school. I didn't like this. I hoped I was going to be a keeper, you see. Ever since I was a boy I wanted to be a keeper but it never happened. 'You won't like it,' they said. 'It is seven days a week and a young lad likes his week-ends off.' I don't know why they said this. They knew I had no Sundays, so to speak. I was in working clothes and round the woods of a Sunday, just as of an ordinary day, so I might just as well have been paid for it. You see, keeping is *the* job for a man who has an eye to nature. There will be something different to look at every day and you'll have never seen it all. But there is no keeper in the village now. The last keeper had the double job of forester and keeper. He had to plant trees when he wasn't feeding pheasants. Whether you can really do both these jobs together, I don't know. There wouldn't be much time to think if you did. You'd have to be two men, which one man can't be if he's to stay honest. But there you are, that's modern demands for you! All the same, keeping would have suited me wonderfully.

I started ploughing, with a reversible plough, when I was eighteen. Somebody took me up to Scarlett Hill and said, 'This handle turns this over, this does something else – and away you go!' I kept straight as I could but I don't trouble so much these days. I don't know why. Because of the plough I suppose. With the old plough you had to have everything marked out and the furrows had to be kept straight if you wanted to finish up any-where at all. The old men criticize. 'That wouldn't have done,' they say. 'You'd have had to have made a better job of it than that when I was a boy – God's truth, you would!' But they forget that they had the labour to do these fine things. There is double the arable in the village and few men wanting to stay and work it, so fancy fine ways aren't needed. The old men will tell you what an interest they took in their tasks – you could call this their main argument. They were brought up on quality work. Now it is quantity work – you've got to cover the ground. I can plough up two acres of the clay land in a day, and more on a light field.

I am a man on my own. I am not interfered with much. I am on the plough and that is where I keep. I am alone nearly all my work time but I can't say that I feel lonely. Not ever, not at all. People say, 'There's Derek, by himself up on that great old field, turning round, going back . . . he's lonely. He must be lonely!' Not at all – and what is 'lonely'? I am watching the whole time, you see. I might have more than a hundred birds in my wake. It is surprisingly interesting. The gulls are with me. But now and then it's nice to see a face and have a chat. Somebody will come past and speak, and that is good. It makes a break. After all, I'm a man and not a bird! But, honestly, if I knew that I was lonely, I'd pack it up tomorrow.

[. . .]

Duncan Campbell · *aged sixty-six* · *sheep-farmer*

A lot of us Scots came to Suffolk between the wars. Things have changed mightily since then; they were tough times. My wife and I have been here for forty-two years. Before this I was a sheep-farmer on the borders of Scotland. My father had a lot of sheep in the Border country. The flocks are very big there. They roam at their own sweet will, as they do in Wales. The hills are where the great art of shepherding is practised, where a man has to work subtly to get the best out of his sheep. They have to 'go over the ground', you see. They like to lie on the driest part of the grazing, which is on the mountain top. So the shepherd has to incline them out all the afternoon and evening in such a way that they reach the top at night. Then, at daybreak, they will leave the tops and gradually drift low into the valleys until they reach the stream. And so they go over all the pasture all the time, over all the hill and valley in one day. And that is the art of good shepherding, to work them gently, to let them go nicely out and in daily. The shepherd will go to his flock in the afternoon, moving straight along the valley to set them out. If there are any slow sheep, he will put his dog round them and gradually they will all slowly walk the little paths they have made on the mountain, one after another, grazing higher and higher, until they reach the top – and sleep. It is a lonely life – my word, it is! A shepherd spends nearly all his life quite alone.

Very few Suffolk farmers keep big flocks now. There were many more sheep when I first arrived. There have been great reductions in East Suffolk, the numbers have gone down by many thousands. It isn't because they are unprofitable but maybe because other animals are easier to farm and offer a better return. One of the reasons why I haven't got so many sheep on my farm is that I am growing sprouts, peas, beans and other things for the frozen food factory. It is these new green crops which have made the wonderful change in the farming round this village. Before these came along, I used to go in for ley farming, taking my leys round the farm, ploughing up after they had been grazed by sheep and cattle every three–four years, and then catching the fertility. I can assure you that, compared with these deep-freeze crops, there isn't a finer way of keeping a farm in a high state of fertility than taking the leys round. It seems *right*. You feel that you are doing things the way they should be done and it makes you glad and satisfied. It surprises me that some people who do not get good root crops don't practise ley farming more. I know hundreds of farmers who would benefit from having a couple of hundred breeding ewes on their land. This present continual serial cropping won't, in the long run, prove so beneficial as a flock of sheep going over the ground every little while. The artificial fertilizers can never give what a flock can give.

The farm was in poor condition when we came here. There was a lot of grass on it, so that was a help. But they had made hay off the same bits of pasture so often – continually hay, hay, hay, imagine that! – that at last they couldn't have got more than a ton per acre. Well, that won't pay, you know. I make very little hay and I'll tell you why. Because you can buy nice hay at £8 10s. a ton. Now if the most you can grow is two tons – why waste the time or run the risk of losing it because of bad weather for £17? We only make hay when it has been a growing year. This was a growing year and we cut acres of beautiful hay.

I missed the mountains when I first came to Suffolk – I still do. My wife and I, we missed the hills and the weir-running streams. I shall always remember these four lines:

> Says old Tom, 'Give me a Border burn
> That can't run without a turn,

And with its bonny babbles
Fills the glens among our native hills . . .'

They were written by J. B. Selkirk. They make me
homesick. I remember saying them for the first time
when I was a young man and standing in a Suffolk field
which was being ploughed with horses by an old man
wearing a long black coat with tail buttons, a bowler hat
and carrying an umbrella! I shall be homesick here, I
thought – and I have been. That old ploughman, he was
a grand old man. So good.

We have farm students now. Just one at a time, and
just for a year's practical work before they go to the
agricultural college. We don't mind what trouble we
have to go to to teach them farming ways, so long as
they make use of all we tell them later on. But some get
tired of it and go into something else. It is disappointing
when this happens. They are usually boys aged about
sixteen. We don't take them into our house; they have
to find lodgings in the village. We give them a turn with
cows, then tractors, reaping, sugar-beeting, everything
as it comes along. The older men sometimes resent the
student. If they do it is because he is putting on airs and
being too clever. He has forgotten how much the older
men know – such wonderful things. Students should
watch their step, keep their eyes open and their mouths
shut. I give them a reference when their year's 'practical'
is up. And they have to make a statement of all that they
have done during the year, what the acreage of the farm
is and what happens on it, the date when they started
the harvest and what machines were used. Many of these

young men get depressed because they can never see any way of getting a farm of their own. They are so dear now. But it was hard for us, too. We young men from Scotland had to struggle along carrying an agricultural ruin on our backs. It is a wonder that any of us can stand upright! I tell the students that farming is three-quarters practical and a quarter theory. And that a farmer must be able to do every job himself before he orders another man to do it. I have the sons of quite well-to-do people as students. I tell them, 'Irrespective of your position, you must be taught to work.'

I am really a shepherd. I could work a dog before I left school. My father would let me have the old ones which were finished for the hills and I would teach them and learn from them. Therefore I got into the art of handling dogs when I was a child, and I've never been without them all my life. And my dogs have always been the Border collie sheep dogs. They are with me in Suffolk and I have trained scores for all the East Anglian farmers, but they come from my homeland. The best of them were registered on both sides of the Border in the nineteenth century and eventually the National Sheep Dog Society, with its own studbook, was founded. They are the best sheep dogs in the world. They say that there are sheep dogs in Wales, but I've never seen a Welsh sheep dog.

A really trained-for-trial-work sheep dog costs between £1–£300 – as much as that! But it will be as valuable as a man on the farm, have no doubt about it. They will even collect cattle if you will let them. I have become an authority on these wonderful animals and have judged the English National Trials on two occasions.

My method is this where training is concerned. I select a puppy from intelligent parents – I am not interested in the puppy if his parents aren't good workers. I feed the puppy well and give him cod liver oil once a week. Then comes the hard part. He loves you now and is all over you the minute you show up, kisses and everything. But he has to learn to stay away from you and it is against his whole nature. You start by getting him to stay still at five yards, then you walk a little farther – 'Now, Ben, sit down – *sit!*' You are taking the frolic out of him and putting the confidence in. After much effort on both your parts he begins to become a sensible dog, instead of jumping and running to no purpose. Once you have taught him stillness you're getting somewhere. When you come to work on the sheep and you can stop them (high short whistle) and make them absolutely still from a distance, then you are getting somewhere. You can stop 'em and start 'em. You have made great progress.

I might work on a dog once or twice a day for a month and after this, when we get to the sheep, the principle is to get the dog to go to the *other* side of the flock. And to get there he must go in such a way as not to disturb the sheep. So if the sheep are in the twelve o'clock position, the dog must start getting to the other side of them from the nine o'clock position. Then he must come round in a curve. Now, how are you going to teach it to do all that? Well, my method is to start the dog off with five sheep placed about fifty yards in front of me. I walk half-way to the sheep leaving the dog motionless. I then

ask him to come round. Naturally, he comes straight, so
I step out towards him as he's rushing past and shout,
'Git out – Git out, Ben!' and before he knows where he
is he's running to the side. Then I whistle him to sit
down. He should be about ten–twenty yards off at the
side of the sheep by now. And then I start to give him
his come-on whistle, or I say, 'Come on up, Ben.' But I
don't let him do this right away. I stop and start him a
number of times. It is a game now and Ben is enjoying
it. There is no dog so anxious to work and to please his
master as a Border collie. Well now, he's gone round
the back of the sheep and bringing them towards you.
You mustn't teach him too much at once. He must do
nothing more than this for a fortnight – just to run out
keeping a nice circle line and bringing a handful of sheep
up to you quietly. Then you teach him flanking, running
to the right or to the left. If the sheep try to escape to
the right you must have a command to make the dog
come round and head them off. A short double high
whistle means 'come to my right' and one long low
whistle means 'come to my left'. You have to give him
encouragement and lots of kindness after each command. And all the time he must be quiet and gentle with
the sheep – never to worry them, you understand. And
there is another important thing. When you have given
a command and the dog begins to respond, never add
another command until he has completed the first one.
And don't repeat the command. So long as he's doing
what you have asked, don't say anything. Never shake
his confidence in any way.

You need to understand sheep; they are very special

animals. Down-bred sheep are very placid and those which come from the hills are timid and wild. Their fright is infectious, it fills the air. It is some old habit which makes them keep together and if there weren't dogs to manage them I don't know what we would all do. I've often said that the British sheep industry would suffer to the extent of a thirty per cent loss if it weren't for the collies. They are the brightest dogs in the world – and all due to the National Sheep Dog Society.

Sheep have to be maintained in a splendid condition, once they begin to go down there is no pulling them up. You have no end of trouble with them if you let them go down. You must understand how to flush them and make them thrive, so that they bring you a good crop of lambs. And how to winter and summer them. And all the time you must do the job as economically as possible, and yet still present them in nice condition at lambing time.

Some East Anglian farmers have no use for sheep at all; others are sheep-minded. They know the value of them on the farm and just wouldn't be without them. Sheep keep a farm in a high state of fertility and also provide a tidy little income. Double purpose creatures, they are.

There is an important sale in Bury St Edmunds during the third week of August and last year I had to come home from holiday in order to get my sheep to it. I had 130 sheep and I took them all. And why? Well, the year before the Queen sent a flock of sheep from Sandringham to this sale – which deals with between 13–14,000 animals altogether – and I saw her get the highest prize. She had sent shearing ewes – ewes which are ready to go to the ram as soon as you get them home and which will lamb in the spring – and they made a lovely pen. Now, I told myself, I would like to beat the Queen. By jove, I looked about and bought a very nice pen of ewe lambs, brought them home, brought them up, took them to the Bury sale the next year and – what do you think? I got the highest price. But only just. I beat Her Majesty by five shillings!

A chap comes up after the sale and says, 'How did you manage it?' Well now, I says quite simply, 'I kept them clear of worms – dosed them in the autumn and again in the spring. I cleared every parasite right out. Then I dosed them for such things as pulpy kidney. I injected them – the scientists have done a tremendous lot for agriculture, make no doubt of it! Things are incredibly better since I started farming years ago – and then I fed these lambs all the winter as economically as I could with sugar-beet pulp, and on the fields before the grass faded and the goodness went out of it. I was never too late or too early with the different cares they needed. I was being a good shepherd. That is how I managed it.'

There is more in the business than making money, you know. I always wanted to be a farmer. I was quite sure. It is a great life. You must praise the land as well as take from it. And order it. There's a field out there – now what have I done to that? I've put humus and nitrogen on it, and now the cows will graze it. I'll fold it twice over and then I'll plough it up, then sow these hand-picked beans. I took over five tons an acre off it this year – two crops in twelve months! The beans go to

Birdseye to be frozen. I am growing eight acres of sprouts for Birdseye. Thirty-two boxes of them left the farm yesterday, and thirty-two the day before. I kept a pedigree herd of cows on only forty-two acres of grass. I add fertilizer to the good natural humus in the grass and freshen it all up with irrigation. The rule with land is to give – then you can take.

The days are better now but people refuse to believe it. I felt quite angry at a meeting in Ipswich the other day. A man got up and read a paper called 'The Countryside through the eyes of the Urban Dweller' – and how he criticized us! Taking down hedges! Putting up ugly buildings! It was awful. We just ignored him. But one man did get up and answer him. He said, 'In spite of all you say, we have still got hedges and the land is fertile, and there is no more beautiful sight than fertile land.' The farmers are thought to lack feelings. I have sometimes accidentally put my big foot on a skylark's nest, eggs and all. It is damn awful – it is you know! 'Clumsy fool brute! *Brute!*' I tell myself. But it is done. Robbie Burns once ploughed-in a mountain daisy and wrote:

> Wee modest crimson-tipped flower
> I've met you in an evil hour
> For I must crush among the stone
> Thy slender stem. To spare thee now
> Is past my power – thou bonny gem!

Have you seen the townspeople in the spring-time, driving out to the lanes and woods, and tearing up the flowers? It is a shocking sight.

William Russ · aged sixty-one · gravedigger

I started digging graves when I was twelve years old and before I left school. I began by helping an old man and by the time I was thirteen I could do the job as well as I can now. I dug graves before my voice broke – there now! People would look down into the hole and see a child. The work didn't upset me; I took it in my stride. Right from a little boy – if Mother was alive she'd be able to tell you – I used to bury guinea-pigs, rabbits, all sorts of things. I had about fifty rabbits and when one died I would make a coffin for it, get my choir surplice from the church vestry and read the Burial Service over it. So burying has been in my blood from a child. I never wanted to do anything else; graves are my vocation.

I've been at the church, official-like, since 1918. I was the legal sexton when I was thirteen and I've buried damn-near the whole of the old village, everyone of them. I remember the first grave I dug. It was for a man named Hayman. I've got all my burials down since the day I started, men, women and children.

So far as funerals are concerned, we've gone from one extreme to the other. Bodies used to be kept in the house for twelve days. Everyone kept the body at home for as long as they could then; they didn't care to part with it, you see. Now they can't get it out quick enough. They didn't like hurrying about anything when I was young, particularly about death. They were afraid that the corpse might still be alive – that was the real reason for hanging on to it. People have a post-mortem now and it's all settled in a minute, but there's no doubt that years ago there were a rare lot of folk who got buried alive. When a sick man passed on the doctor was told, but he never came to look at the corpse. He just wrote out the death certificate. People always made a point of leaving an instruction in their wills to have a vein cut. Just to be on the safe side.

There was an old man near Framlingham, old Micah Hibble, he was laid out for dead three times. The last time he was actually in his coffin and waiting for the funeral to begin. When I asked, 'Anymore for a last look before he's screwed down?' there was the usual nuisance pushing his way through the mourners and saying, 'Yes, I do!' Trust somebody to get you fiddling about and making the funeral late. The bell was going, so you know how late it was. Anyway, when this man looked in the coffin he saw that Micah had moved. Well do you know, he recovered! And what's more, he is supposed to have written a book about what he saw, although I've never set eyes on it. He reckoned he saw Heaven and Hell but he wouldn't say what he saw in Hell; he thought it would be too much for Framlingham. He lived for years after this.

And there was this old lady at Wickham Market and she was in three different coffins. They called her Cheat-the-grave at last. All these things happened because people will insist on checking on death with a mirror, which isn't a mite of good. The only way is to stick a shred of cotton-wool where the lips part and if there's the least little wind of life it will flutter. I can always tell if a person is dead by looking at the eyes. I never make a mistake about dead eyes. I see at once when the seeing has gone.

Village folk have been buried over and over again in the same little bits of churchyard. You have to throw somebody out to get somebody in – three or four sometimes. I always put all the bones back so that they lie tidy-like just under the new person. They're soon all one. The parson said to me, 'How is it that you get so many in one grave?' and I always tell him that I must have disturbed a plague pit. Parsons will believe anything.

The rich people are buried in vaults, you know. I had to open a vault the other day and put a woman in. She joined six or seven others and I had to shove 'em over and say, 'Come you together now, make room for a little 'un!' Vaults are sweet places. Everybody lies in lead first, then wood, so there's no smell. I went into the vault at Stanton when Lord Eastham's wife died. It was full and I had to lay her on the floor because her relations had all the shelves. It was first come, first served. The coffins were all made of panelled oak, great black things as black as a fireplace. Good God, they last for generations!

I've dug for all denominations, from Catholic to Plymouth Brethren. The chapel people are the worst. First of all they're a good three quarters of an hour in the chapel while the preacher spouts about the dead man and estimates whether he's saved, and then, when they get to the grave, on it goes again. There's no end to it. They forget we all knew the corpse. And then, when they're none too sure about the saving, you should hear them then! There was Jed's funeral – well we don't need any telling about Jed! Well Jed might have been a bad lot but he wasn't a bad sort. You know. I mean he was Jed, wasn't he? Well, this chapel preacher stood there by the hole I had got ready for Jed and was as near as damn-it saying that Jed wasn't saved although he *hoped* he was. So after the funeral I went up to him and said, 'My God, you've had some talk about Jed, haven't you? I know you're here to say a few words – but you've said too much!' I said, 'Do you reckon that *you* are saved?' He said, 'I hope so.' 'Very well then,' I said, 'but do you remember when you get in front of your Maker he won't ask you what Jed has done – he'll ask what you've been up to.' You could see he didn't like it.

The parsons aren't much better. But there, you don't find many *parsons* now. Only men who have done their life's work serving as a colonel or a schoolmaster and then get themselves ordained. I don't really call these people parsons. I don't mince my words with them. When you bury between 180–200 people a year you can afford to be honest.

Dust to dust they say. It makes me laugh. Mud to mud, more like. Half the graves round here are waterlogged. Foxton is a terrible wet place; the moment you get the grass off, you're in the water. I float grass on the water so the mourners can't see it but when the coffin is lowered it has to be held under with a pole until you can get a bit of heavy soil on top of it. At Dearburgh the graves fill up to within eight inches of the top. I've drawn as much as fifty pails of water out of a grave at Dearburgh, the last when the funeral was coming up the path. And still the coffin had to be held under three feet of it. It all comes down from the cricket pitch.

The bodies are washed and dressed in shrouds. Except for a parson, and he's buried in his robes. When you bury a parson you always bury him 're incumbent' – the opposite way to everybody else. Everybody lies with their feet to the east so that when they rise they face the Lord. But a parson, you see, you bury him with his feet to the west, so that when he rises he faces his flock. And serve him right, I say. I had a bit of bother about this once.

An old canon had died and was cremated, and the ashes were kept until his wife passed on. I put the jar of ashes on the wife's coffin and lowered the two together. Well, of course, as everybody knows, all that family, particularly the daughters, were over-educated. They were old maids. They weren't cranky because they hadn't had a man but because they'd had too many old books. Their brains were strained. Well, a month after I had buried her mother's corpse and her father's ashes, along comes Miss Bolt to my house to kick up hell. 'You haven't buried Father right,' she says. 'Oh?' I says. 'You knew he should have been buried re incumbent,' she says. 'What *are* you talking about, Miss Bolt?' I say. 'I put your Father's urn on your Mother's coffin, and if you can tell me the difference between the way I put him and the way you want him, I'll dig him up and turn him round.' So then she says that I should have turned her mother the other way round as the reverend was on top of her! I mean if parsons' wives are going to get themselves buried re incumbent, where's it going to stop?

We've got a man in the churchyard named Tyler. He used to be secretary to the golf club. When he died he was buried facing south so that when he rises he can see the links. And it was done! I told the parson, 'If a person of my walk of life expressed a wish like that, you'd say I was qualified for the tall chimney' [St Audrey's Mental Hospital].

I never had any qualms about my work. When I was young I delighted in death. The funerals were big and grand and slow. You learnt a lot about everybody. They crept about in the deepest black – now they come to a funeral in all the colours of the rainbow. And afterwards they don't even walk up to the churchyard to cart the dead flowers away. They have one word for the dead when they have got them into the ground, and that is 'forgotten'. I tell them, too. They're upset, but it's the truth. They'll put a stone up with a 'There you are, we've done all we can for you, now bugger you!' They'll even put crazy paving on top of the grave so they don't have to pay me to clip the grass. And the price of it all! When I started you could get coffin, wreaths and everything for £5 – you could actually get a coffin for 30s. Now you wouldn't buy a coffin for a stillborn for under three quid. As for an adult's, it will cost you between £40–50.

And talking of money, I must mention the Table of Fees. Each church has got a Table of Fees which says where the money should go at a funeral. There is the incumbent with his price, there is the clerk with his price and there is the sexton with his price. You would think it was plain enough but I have to read the damn thing aloud to half the parsons or they'd diddle me out of a mint of money. When I do a funeral I'm entitled to 10s. for the service in the church – any church. I don't often get this because the parson takes it. Of course you could argue around this because the Table of Fees says, 'Where no clerk or sexton is employed the incumbent can take the money' – which of course is fair enough up to a point. But believe me when it comes to *little* money matters, parsons are the biggest swindlers on earth. They are. They're that quick on the small change you don't see the passing of it. The burial fees are terrible. It costs a £10 church fee for a parishioner to be buried at Weston – in his own churchyard!

Every parson you come into contact with will have different ways about death. You can't keep 'em in order, you know, these damned parsons! They'll all think different if they can. They'll either cut things out of the Burial Service or stuff things in. It's no use giving the mourners a book so they can follow what is going on. Now old Canon Watson, he'd give you the Service, no more and no less. But the majority of parsons use the 1928 version – which, I agree, is much more cheerful. There's nothing in it like that bit of Job where it talks about the skin worms destroying the body, for instance. Nor that bit about corruption from Corinthians. They say these things are morbid. Well they *are* morbid. It is what people need when they are staring down at the grave-dirt.

It's the same with the Litany. I said to the old Bishop, 'How often could you walk into a church now and hear the Litany read? Or the Athanasian Creed – and that should be said at least three times a year!' 'Ho! ho!' says he, 'it's all out of date.' I said, 'What was good enough for your forefathers should be good enough for you.' 'Ho! ho!' he says.

The clergy don't stick to religion as we knew it. They do things that are forbidden. They are pulling the Bible to pieces. Altering, altering . . . I said to the Bishop, 'What do you think of parsons, my lord?' He said, 'What do you?' I said, 'Well they don't preach hellfire. They used to, why don't they now?' He said, 'What, are you blaming the parsons?' 'Certainly,' I said. 'All these parsons preach is the love of God. But they leave out the wrath. What is the use of love without wrath? Tell me that.' I said, 'You are told what will happen to you if you obey His will, so it is only fair that you should know what will happen to you if you don't.' People aren't frightened any more, that is the trouble. If they had to do my work they would know that life is a frightening business. I had a parson say to me the other day, as I was digging a grave, 'Do you think these people will ever come out there again, Tender?' I said, 'They'll have a damned job after I've finished with them!' He said, seriously, 'Once you're in there, you're finished.' 'Never!' I said. But we don't know, do we? We've just got to leave the body after it has been covered up. The people I've accidentally smashed to pieces in my time, they're going to have a rum time of it.

I'll tell you what I think. In the Burial Service it tells you that when you are dead you go into the earth like a grain but it doesn't say anything about your coming out in the same form as you went in. You might come back as a cat! I love cats. I have a family of ten cats in the churchyard. They used to sleep cold among the tombs but I've made a little hole in the charnel door and now they're very comfortable indeed. They cost me 10s. a week to feed and they don't even belong to me. They don't belong to anybody. They watch the funerals from afar off. It's a healthy life for them. There are worse things than coming back as a cat.

I'm not a Christian. I do a lot of things I shouldn't do, so I can't count myself as one. Life isn't as comfortable as it used to be. Nobody wants to know you. I have been widowed for ten years. I go to church every Sunday but nobody speaks to me unless they want something. Snobbish. They're all snobs now. I'm not blowing my own trumpet, but almost ever since I was born I have been at everybody's beck and call. I have no family, none at all. No one in all the world is my relation. I never did read a lot. I never could give my mind to it. I talk too much, that is my failing. I come into contact with many people at a serious time, so I have picked up serious conversation. What most folk have once or twice in a lifetime, I have every day. I want to be cremated and my ashes thrown in the air. Straight from the flames to the winds, and let that be that.

THE STORY OF PENGUIN CLASSICS

Before 1946 ...'Classics' are mainly the domain of academics and students, without readable editions for everyone else. This all changes when a little-known classicist, E. V. Rieu, presents Penguin founder Allen Lane with the translation of Homer's Odyssey that he has been working on and reading to his wife Nelly in his spare time.

1946 The Odyssey becomes the first Penguin Classic published, and promptly sells three million copies. Suddenly, classic books are no longer for the privileged few.

1950s Rieu, now series editor, turns to professional writers for the best modern, readable translations, including Dorothy L. Sayers's *Inferno* and Robert Graves's *The Twelve Caesars*, which revives the salacious original.

1960s 1961 sees the arrival of the Penguin Modern Classics, showcasing the best twentieth-century writers from around the world. Rieu retires in 1964, hailing the Penguin Classics list as 'the greatest educative force of the 20th century'.

1970s A new generation of translators arrives to swell the Penguin Classics ranks, and the list grows to encompass more philosophy, religion, science, history and politics.

1980s The Penguin American Library joins the Classics stable, with titles such as *The Last of the Mohicans* safeguarded. Penguin Classics now offers the most comprehensive library of world literature available.

1990s Penguin Popular Classics are launched, offering readers budget editions of the greatest works of literature. Penguin Audiobooks brings the classics to a listening audience for the first time, and in 1999 the launch of the Penguin Classics website takes them online to an ever larger global readership.

The 21st Century Penguin Classics are rejacketed for the first time in nearly twenty years. This world famous series now consists of more than 1,300 titles, making the widest range of the best books ever written available to millions – and constantly redefining the meaning of what makes a 'classic'.

The Odyssey continues ...

The best books ever written

PENGUIN CLASSICS

SINCE 1946